Secrets and Lies

Memoir of the Kennedy Years

Tiger Iron Press

Macon, Georgia, USA

For Tamera, my new sweet friend, walking in the footsteps of her charming mother.

I hope after reading this you will still be talking to me.

George B. Mettler

1-25-2013

Secrets and Lies

Memoir of the Kennedy Years

By a Reluctant Witness
George B. Mettler
Former Special Agent, FBI

Tiger Iron Press

All art work in this book created by author George B. Mettler

With the exception of the photographs of George B. Mettler, all photographs can be found on the Internet, and are in the public domain. Wikipedia also has the official portrait of Kennedy by Arron Shider and another Kennedy portrait by Abbie Rowe.

Cover design by Julianne Gleaton, www.juliannedesign.com

Book design by E. Michael Staman, Mike.Staman@TigerIronPress.com

Library of Congress Cataloging-in-Publication Data
Secrets and Lies: Memoir of the Kennedy Years / George B. Mettler
ISBN 978-0-9851745-0-7

Search by: 1. Nonfiction. 2. John F. Kennedy. 3. Kennedy assassination. 4. Bay of Pigs. 5. Implications of the deaths of John and Robert Kennedy. 6. Memoir, Hoover and the FBI. 7. Mafia.

First Edition: 2012

Printed in the United States of America

Dedication

This book is for my late wife, Darlene, my dearest companion of forty years and my everlasting inspiration, and for our sons J.D. and Sean, with love and gratitude from the stranger in their house.

Acknowledgements

I would like to thank A. Louise Staman, Editor and CEO of Tiger Iron Press, without whose steadfast help and generosity this book would have been another decade in the making. In addition, I thank the technical magician at Tiger Iron, Mike Staman, and Karen Staman, editor extraordinaire, for her diligence beyond the lines of duty, and her unfailing advice in all details.

I am also thankful to all of my family and friends, including the members of our Thursday night writers' club, all of whom have stood beside me throughout the years with unqualified encouragement. The insights and support of this group have proved invaluable as *Secrets and Lies* evolved.

I also must give special thanks to my late wife, Darlene, without whose loving encouragement there would likely have been no book at all.

TABLE OF CONTENTS

Editor's Note

Probably no one has personally known as many people directly or indirectly associated with the assassination of President John F. Kennedy as George B. Mettler. The situation of his life, his residences and his career choices provided exclusive entrance into the world and people surrounding this monstrous act. As a result, Mettler sheds new light on the factors that led to and resulted in the Kennedy assassination. In this memoir Mettler "connects the dots," exposing corruption and deceit at the highest levels of American government and providing a new perspective on the life, times, and death of John Kennedy.

At the request of his wife, George Mettler put down in words what he learned as a Special Agent in the FBI and in other unique positions. It was her dying wish; she made him promise, and here in *Secrets and Lies: Memoir of the Kennedy Years* is the result: a memoir reluctantly written, a promise kept, and a tardy if historically required presentation of the life and death of John F. Kennedy.

It is fleshed out by pictures and Mettler's own paintings, capturing one of the darkest times in American history. In meticulous detail George Mettler presents the personages of this drama, some in stark detail, shows the mistakes of the Warren Commission, and explains how our present-day experiences have been shaped by the awful past.

The result is a shocking, enlightening, exposé.

A. Louise Staman
Editor and CEO
Tiger Iron Press

Preface

Shortly before she died in March, 2008, my wife whispered my name. "George."

"I'm here, Sugar-Girl." At her hospice bedside I leaned closer but was careful not to touch her in a way that would cause her pain. Her fifteen-year ordeal with cancer of the breast, spine and brain had left her in recent years a near-paraplegic. Now sight and speech were waning daily.

"Look at me," she whispered in her paper-thin voice. "What if you were to get like this and hadn't accomplished the work you were meant to do ... because you had used as an excuse your obligations to me?"

I was speechless. Where had the words and the energy come from?

"I would know, you must realize that. I would know I had failed you. You must grieve for a time and then you must get on with your life; you must accomplish the work you are meant to do. How many people have lived a life like yours? How many have known the characters you have known, had the adventures you have experienced in so many exotic locations throughout the world?"

She paused for breath. "And how many people have personal knowledge of as-yet undisclosed facts surrounding the assassination of President Kennedy?"

She tried to reach up and wipe the tears from my face but the effort proved too much. She drew a deep breath and spoke the last words she ever uttered: "Promise. Promise you will spend the rest of your life in search of your literary voice and your artistic vision. *Promise?*"

I promised.

Jack and Jacqueline Kennedy

PROLOGUE

Tampa, Florida
November 17, 1963

Street-talk was rampant that JFK was going to be hit. Many of my friends and informants had assured me that hit teams had been selected and were in place. But did any of these guys know what they were talking about?

The president would be clipped the next morning, they said, during his motorcade here in Tampa. And if it didn't come off as planned, he would be shot later in the day in Miami during an extension of his Florida campaign swing. And if not in Miami, then for certain on the 22nd when he went to Dallas to satisfy Vice President Johnson's ostensible desire to have him bolster Democratic chances in the upcoming Texas elections.

"An' you don' watch your ass, cracker, dey goin' clip *you,* too."

"What the hell are you talking about?"

"Don' play innocent wit' me. Dey try shuttin' you down wit' da phone smear. It was a message. Knock it off, see, play ball, rejoin the team or else. Shit, man. Phone calls, anonymous letters. Who you think you are there, fuckin' Paul Revere? *Anonymous* hell, dey on to you, Georgie. An' dey won' let you get away wit' it."

It was shortly before midnight. We were talking in one of our secure meeting spots in back-alley darkness off of Seventh Avenue in Ybor City, Tampa's exotic Latin Quarter. A discordant symphony of Latin music wafted in the breeze from the clubs, bars and restaurants in the neighborhood. Like a pair of furtive lovers, we were hunkered down in the cool autumn freshness on the front seat of my 1958 Pontiac.

"Boots" Ruiz had been one of my good friends since the playground baseball days of our childhood here in the semi-tropical city by the bay. He was called Boots as a result of all the second base grounders he consistently booted. But we weren't children any more. I was a disillusioned ex-FBI agent and a congressman's former law associate with a recently tarnished reputation, and my buddy was a mob hit man whose own days in the game were numbered.

"Never mind me," I told him with lofty self-abnegation, "the president is my concern. How the hell can they expect to get

3

away with it? Surely Santo won't let it happen, not here, not in his own hometown."

Santo Trafficante Jr. was the reputed Mafia strongman in Tampa, Miami and Havana, Cuba. He assumed godfather status following the 1954 death of his father, Santo Trafficante Sr., from natural causes. My FBI contacts had informed me — off the record, of course — that the present plan to hit Kennedy was a

Mafia scheme all the way. It had been devised and organized by Carlos Marcello of New Orleans, Johnny Roselli of Chicago and Santo Trafficante. The Mafia, it seems, had decided that this was the only way to quash the prosecutorial zeal of Attorney General Robert Kennedy. Marcello, in fact, was presently on trial in a New Orleans federal court in the government's effort to exile him permanently from the United States as an undesirable alien.

S. Trafficante Jr.   The Mafia planners were certain that details of the murder of the president would be smothered under a deep government cover-up, with no finger of involvement or guilt pointed at them. At the present time, however, I was unaware of these reasons for mob feelings of security.

I was well aware that Santo and the Mafia were *not* the only cast members in this malevolent drama. Roselli was a long-time CIA asset and was involved with the Agency in a separate plot to assassinate Fidel Castro. And Santo was often on the Company help list too. Whatever this pair knew, their Agency cronies also knew. There was no doubt in my mind that the CIA was complicit in the Mafia plot to kill JFK and knew what was happening at every step of the way.

Boots kept on like he wasn't even listening to me. "Be a turkey shoot, see. High-powered rifles from a couple hi-rise buildings, another shot from a frontal position, an' a patsy left behind to take the rap an' then be nailed in his attempt to escape."

"Who the hell would be so stupid as to ...?"

"Got designated patsies here in Tampa, down in Miami, and over in Dallas. It's all set, man. I tell you, it's fuckin' on."

I was breathless. "Jesus, are *you* one of the …?"

But I couldn't ask it. And I didn't really want to know if he was one of the designated shooters. I wouldn't have gotten an answer from him anyway.

Suddenly, he slapped me on the arm with his rolled cap and jumped out of the car.

"Watch you'self, babe," he said in a voice choked with emotion as he merged into the enveloping shadows.

I never saw him again. He was arrested on a murder charge some years later, convicted and sentenced to life in prison, where he died.

Monday morning, November 18, 1963, dawned clear and sultry, and I was a basket case. I'd had fewer than three hours sleep. Once again, I'd sent anonymous telephone warnings to the FBI office in Tampa, Bureau HQ in Washington, to Attorney General Robert Kennedy's office, the Secret Service, a number of former FBI colleagues on and off active duty, and to a variety of media sources.

But my friend was right, like the many other colleagues and trusted informants I'd talked with in the preceding days, weeks and months, no one was listening, not even the local media. It seemed that no one wanted to acknowledge these warning bells and whistles of alarm. Nothing, they all said, could be done in any case. It was too late. The train had left the station, and there were no road blocks in its path.

My apartment building faced the road that the presidential motorcade would use, and my balcony overlooked the scene with an unimpeded view. In spite of all the warnings, mine and many others, I was stunned that no visible security precautions had been taken along this section of the parade route. My information at this point in time was limited. But I wondered where the military Presidential Protection Unit was. It would be some weeks before I learned what had happened to them. Unsecured windows and balconies overflowed with waiting gawkers, numbering presidential partisans and opponents in unequal measure. Most people in the Tampa Bay area had been Nixon supporters in the last election.

Now, at the last moment, I wriggled into my shoulder holster, slipped on a windbreaker to cover the bulge, and ran downstairs and across the vacant field toward the roadway with no clear idea as to what I might do. The road, originally known as Lafayette Street and more recently as Grand Central Avenue, was soon to be renamed John F. Kennedy Boulevard in honor of the president's visit.

It was a lovely day of autumn sunshine with a mild breeze off nearby Old Tampa Bay. It was almost like a Gasparilla parade day, the annual event that brought thousands of spectators, pirates from the invasion ships lying at anchor in the harbor, and marauding brigands into the streets. There were spectators on both sides of the road now, waving, laughing, cheering and jeering. But today there were real pirates and cutthroats among the roiling crowd, and murder most foul was their mission.

There was no visible security, no Secret Service, no military presidential protection personnel; nothing of the sort was in evidence. This was not the work of Santo Trafficante or any other Mafioso. They didn't have this kind of power. Arrangements of *this* nature had to have been coordinated by official complicity.

And my informants had told me that the Mafia plan was to shoot Kennedy from an unprotected window in a high-rise hotel in downtown Tampa when the motorcade slowed in front of the hotel to make a sharp left turn; the kill weapon would be a high-powered rifle with a telescopic sight. Even an adequate marksman couldn't miss the target, and the shooters would be international marksmen with impeccable records.

As I reached the sidewalk, the presidential limousine drew abreast of my position, having obviously completed the downtown portion of the motorcade without incident. I was relieved to see that at least there were four Secret Service agents trotting alongside the vehicle. But none of the agents had taken positions on the bumpers, and the bubble top was down.

Riding in the backseat were President Kennedy and Sam Gibbons. Mr. Sam was my friend and former employer and was now a respected United States Congressman. Mr. Sam saw me and waved, and then I think he nudged the president and whispered something to him. Kennedy looked over at me, beamed his brilliant smile, and waved.

I was no more than a few feet away and took the opportunity to shout: *"Buena suerte*, Mr. President! Good luck."

I could also have taken the opportunity to place a number of hollow-point rounds in and about his head and upper body extremities.

But, as the world knows, President Kennedy left the city unharmed later that day en route to Miami. By sundown, however, I was a shattered wreck, drinking straight gin in the shadows of my balcony while reliving the events of the day over and over, with repetitious images coming at me like those of a broken film reel in an empty theater. The president had made his speeches in Tampa and had departed the city unmolested. No amount of drink, however, would block the horrifying scenario that played out over and again in my mind with frightening clarity.

There were three shots fired in rapid sequence, and the president and the congressman were dead, as was the patsy who was immediately shot and killed by fast-acting Secret Service agents who then discovered the murder weapon in the deceased culprit's possession. The killer was a native Tampan who had long been acquainted with men known to have been in the forefront of such murderous intentions. He was an alleged renegade FBI agent who had conspired on sacred soil with Cuban exiles, their mobster associates, and corrupt CIA handlers to assassinate the leader of a foreign nation. Fidel Castro, however, had survived the nefarious plots, and President Kennedy had been killed in his stead.

In my drunken delirium I could hear the gunfire, see the frantic commotion and *feel* the bullets ripping through my body. But, thankfully, history had not evolved in that manner. Fate had decreed that John F. Kennedy would keep a rendezvous with death on another day in another city with another patsy on the mark.

A patsy named Lee Harvey Oswald, whom I had known when we were boys in New Orleans, when the world was young.

November 22, 2010.

Private bulletin: I'm writing this at my desk all tucked snugly away in my home in the Georgia woods. I can't help thinking about all that happened in detail, as I have done on this date every year since 1963. I always try to comprehend just how different our country and the world would be were it not for the tragic events of that long-ago day. Do you remember? Events that should never have been allowed to occur. Criminal events that to this day have never been sufficiently examined. JFK deserved better. The country and the world deserve better.

J. Edgar Hoover

PART ONE

The Brotherhood

Gee, but I'd like to be a G-Man and go Bang! Bang! Bang! Bang!
Just like Dick Tracy, what a "he-man," And go Bang! Bang! Bang! Bang!
I'd do as I please, act high-handed and regal
'Cause when you're a G-Man, there's nothing illegal.

From "When I Grow Up"
(The G-Man Song)
By Harold Rome
Pins and Needles, 1937

Southern Illinois, 1962

I was twenty-eight years old in the autumn of 1962. I'd been with the Bureau for less than a year and had never killed or even fired a live round at a human target or committed a felony. I didn't know it yet but I would never again walk with such innocence. It was after 2 a.m. as I and two colleagues crept along the darkened alley, our footsteps crunching softly against the light snow cover. Two of us took up watch positions at opposite ends of the alley, while the third man picked the lock in a narrow wooden door.

When we got inside the building, we moved carefully but knowingly in the darkness of the dining area. We'd cased the joint for weeks and knew exactly the layout and routine of the staff. We had little more than an hour to set the bug, do a quick plaster-and-patch job and get out before the morning shift would arrive at one of the most popular lunch and night spots in town located near the border of East St. Louis.

The restaurant was owned by the most powerful Mafioso in the southern part of Illinois, and his operation was our target. (Many names used in the course of this memoir are fictional and/or composites of real names. I do this to protect the innocent and to conceal guilt.) This guy was tough and brutal, and his word in southern Illinois was law. He used the restaurant and the booth for some of the family's most private talks. We intended to sit in on them.

I assumed a lookout position in the front window, and Gene Elliott stood guard at the back door while the technical expert sent out from SOG — Seat of Government, as J. Edgar Hoover ostentatiously referred to FBI Headquarters in Washington, D.C. — got to work. The guy had been pulling illicit black-bag jobs for the director for twenty years. I hoped this job would not be his last. And all it would take was for a cook, a janitor, or one of the wiseguys to come strolling in early for a change. But Gene had assured us that it almost never happened.

"But what if it does?" I'd asked earlier. "What do we do then?"

He'd pointed his finger at me, smiled craftily and said, "Bang, bang."

"And if the local cops catch us? They know nothing about us, we carry no identification, what if they ...?"

"Bang, bang."

I'd laughed then, but I wasn't laughing now. The techie opened his leather satchel and dug out his work tools. This was my first big undercover job, and I had little experience to fall back on. The classroom instruction in new agent's training school meant little once you were out in the field. Oh, I'd run the gamut of ordinary case work that all new agents are initially exposed to: applicant cases, stolen car investigations, fugitive cases, the occasional bank robbery, and a file folder full of security cases. The latter were mostly background investigations of suspected Communist sympathizers.

Director Hoover would tolerate no slip-shod pursuit of extreme threats to the security of the United States, but organized crime investigations had been of slight interest to the director over the years. The impetus behind this present-day pursuit of the mob flowed from Robert Kennedy, the U.S. Attorney General and Hoover's boss. It made for a touchy situation for us street agents.

The techie drilled noiselessly into the wall beside the target booth, using the narrow beam of a small pin flashlight like a lighted cigar clamped between his teeth. He set the mike — an object the size of an orange — and then ran an attached wire up inside the wall into the waiting hands of a colleague on the second floor of the building. My mouth gummed up, and my heart hammered so hard in my chest that I feared the noise would reveal our mendacity to the entire town.

But I was more excited than I'd ever been in my life. By God, I was a G-man!

A month passed and the bug was working fine, but so far the take had been of little or no value. The whole operation seemed like a sham out of an old black-and-white cops-and-robbers movie. Our cast of players on the undercover team starred six agents and an array of electronic gadgetry that I barely knew how to operate. We maintained a covert office nearby, and it was another cold wet night when I climbed the stairs to relieve Gene Elliot from duty in the audio room.

"What's hot?" I asked, glancing over his shoulder at the surveillance log.

"Same old wiseguy horseshit. Fucking and killing, before and after. Couple local pols came by earlier, that bent sheriff's deputy, and that goddamned shanty priest on the mooch for another bingo handout."

He got up, stretched, and handed me the headgear. I had him by three inches, but Gene, an Iowa farm boy, outweighed me by twenty pounds. He had a good record at HQ and a better reputation among his colleagues in the field. He was the senior agent on this undercover caper. I'd served two years as an Army officer but was a lawyer too, and I was uncomfortable about the illegal operation we were running, even one that had been devised by other lawyers more learned and experienced than I. Hoover was a lawyer. And Robert Kennedy, the Attorney General. We were all lawyers and breaking the law together.

I'd been shocked to discover the extra-legal extent that the government went to in its newly energized campaign against organized crime. I'd discovered corruption, deceit and some honor in the Mafia, as well as duplicity, incompetence and gross illegality in the government, often at the highest levels, which were sworn to uphold the law and defend the Constitution. The FBI couldn't be excluded from this latter group. I didn't know it then, but my education was just beginning.

I agreed in principle with the goal of Attorney General Robert Kennedy's CIP — the Criminal Intelligence Program. But in doing the job, I realized that our tactics were often as despicable as those of the targets of our investigation. The methods included a relentless physical and electronic surveillance, wiretapping, surreptitious entries — known as "black-bag jobs" — and mail intercepts, etc., all of which were illegal and unconstitutional.

I placed my sidearm on the table while Gene packed his gear for the shift change. The tape was rolling, recording everything that was said downstairs in the target booth.

Until recently, the Bureau had shown little interest in the activities of the so-called Mafia. Director Hoover had on numerous public occasions even denied the very existence of such a syndicated organization. All of his interest — his obsession, many said — was focused on the pernicious spread of international Communism.

In view of this careless FBI attitude, American mobsters, although reasonably careful about their homes and offices — and to some extent their cars — for some inexplicable reason believed that they were safe in their private watering holes.

In our target restaurant, no patrons were allowed to approach the special padded booth situated beside the swinging kitchen door uninvited, a booth that our surveillance team hoped would soon convey its occupants to a special iron-padded suite of cells in a federal penitentiary.

Gene slipped into a lined windbreaker and was anxious to go. "There was some talk about the *padron* stopping by for a steak on his way home from a conference in Chicago," he said, indicating the rolling tape.

"Think we'll ever get to meet him up close and personal?"

"Meet him in court someday, that's what this caper's all about."

"I just hope *we're* not the ones who wind up in the dock."

"Jaysus, kid! You got to stop stewing about all this or it'll drive you bonkers." He stuck a cold stogie between his teeth.

"Okay," I said reluctantly, "but is *this* the best answer we've got?" I indicated our secret cubicle, which was jam-packed with the latest state-of-the-art electronic gadgetry on loan from the technical division at SOG.

"Best answer we got right now." Gene chuckled, spread his legs and enthusiastically hustled his nuts. "One hot mike can be worth a hundred agents in the field. Just look what we got out of the blabbermouth up in Chicago last month. Jaysus! Asshole laid out the entire structure of the national crime syndicate in one thirty-minute conversation. Identified wiseguys we'd never heard of. Like the ones from the Deep South. No idea, until now, how influential they are in the larger scheme of things."

I wasn't about to open this can of worms. The blabbermouth that he was referring to was none other than Sam Giancana, acting head of the Chicago Outfit. I had a lot of friends in Chicago from college days, friends who knew things. And some of the names that Gene was talking about were people I'd heard about or known for most of my life.

"Okay," I conceded, "bugging is one thing, but breaking-and-entering is something else. We can't even use any of this stuff in court."

"What we know can be a lot more important than what we can use in court." Gene finished off the last of the cold coffee and shuttered like a dog shedding water. "Jaysus! Tha's wonnerful stuff!"

"Look, Gene ..." I had more to say, but he quickly cut me off.

"Look, kid, we do the best we can. We hitch up our pants and follow orders."

"We don't ever think for ourselves? No personal responsibility for our actions? If it please the court, Your Honor, we were just following orders."

"One of the hazards of the trade, kid. We live by the 11th Commandment: Thou shalt not get caught."

I just wasn't buying it. "No, we've got to abide by the rules ourselves, or the whole system will come down around our ears."

He shrugged and started for the door. "But *you* don't have to worry about any of these things — the Boss knows what he's doing."

"That's just it, I'm not sure that he does."

Gene turned back, and his face went red. "Now wait a damn minute, hot shot! You weren't here when Mr. Hoover started the ball rolling. I don't care what went on in the old days, after Apalachin he took off the restraints."

We'd studied the episode in our training class at Quantico. An incident in the sleepy upstate New York hamlet of Apalachin in 1957 was one of the most colossal blunders in the history of organized crime. More than a hundred big-name racketeers had gathered in conclave at a member's supposedly secure rural farmstead with a full agenda of mob interests to be addressed. But the business of the day was rudely interrupted when a unit of the state police unexpectedly appeared on the scene. Notably, Hoover and the FBI were in no way involved.

In one of the most comic-opera episodes in underworld legend, a hoard of aging gangsters — a few of whom I had known in my youth; an element of my past that I'd so-far kept to myself — wearing their custom-tailored suits and polished alligator shoes suddenly bailed out of the rambling two-story farmhouse by way of windows, doors, cellar-hatches and any other opening they could cram their corpulent bodies through. Once in the open, they scattered like hens-a-loping, crashing frantically through the surrounding woods, bushes and brambles.

A few escaped apprehension; most did not. And although no charges or convictions were sustained in the aftermath — a meeting of citizens is not a Constitutional violation — it was a public relations disaster for the mob. Even the foot-dragging Hoover was forced to abandon his see-no-evil posture regarding an organized criminal enterprise in America. His reluctant response was the creation of the Bureau's Top Hoodlum Program.

"Okay, I know about the THP. But I can't help thinking that Hoover still wouldn't go after the mob if Bobby wasn't chewing on his ass seven days a week. I hear the talk among the old-timers up in Springfield (our field office headquarters was located in the state capital) that for almost forty years the director had done little or nothing concerning the Mafia. And now, with all of this high-tech snooping — his idea or Bobby's orders? — we seem to have gone from one extreme to the other."

Gene nodded. "For God, mother and country, amen."

"I'm not even convinced the A.G. knows what we're doing."

"Are you kidding? You heard him the other night, snarling like a rabid dog."

Robert Kennedy, unlike so many other government agency heads, was a hands-on administrator. He was likely to show up at any hour and demand a detailed briefing on your operation. He was in and out of Chicago with some regularity and had visited with us twice in the federal building over in East St. Louis.

"He's a roll of rusty barbed wire, all right. 'That was good work, men. But all of that was yesterday. What about the rest of today and tomorrow?'" Gene laughed at the impersonation, and I hurried on while I still had his attention. "I know he listens to what we say, and reads our reports, but we label all this stuff informant material. That doesn't reveal *how* we get the information. I'll bet Hoover's never told him about our black bag jobs, the illegal taps and bugs, and you sure can't convince me that all this sleaze has been authorized by the president."

Gene brushed a hand over his neatly cropped hair and pulled a deep sigh up out of his socks. "You got a hell of a lot to learn about knights in shining armor. Jack wasn't so goddamned pure he wouldn't accept all those bogus votes that Giancana and the Daley crew stole in Chicago, votes that ensured his election."

"There's no proof of all those allegations," I protested lamely.

Gene shrugged and tried unsuccessfully to get his cigar lighted. "Okay, kid, I don't want to fight with you. But take a piece of advice from an old dog in the kennel and don't make up your mind about folks too quick. If you can't see what's going on — all those stolen votes, Sinatra and his bunch of Hollywood perverts playing footsies with the Brothers K, Giancana and the bimbo he's sharing with ..."

"*Now that's* bullshit, Gene, and you know it!" I didn't want to believe it; I just couldn't believe it. The president shacking up with a Mafia bimbo. JFK was the most important reason I'd come into the Bureau. 'Ask not what your country can do for you. Ask what you can do for your country.' I took his words to heart, in the face of considerable opposition from family, friends and associates.

Gene gave me a sour look. "You just don't want to believe anything bad about your fair-haired hero, but you don't mind listening to all the filthy garbage circulating about the director."

"Now that's not true!" I protested, stung to the quick by the accusation. "I *am* loyal to Mr. Hoover. I've been devoted to him and to his G-men all of my life." But I knew what he was referring to, having heard all the rumors. In many groups — inside the Bureau and out — J. Edgar Hoover, in addition to being a corrupt, self-centered bully, was reputed to be a homosexual pervert of the first-order. Quietly, such things were said.

"Well, you got a peculiar way of showing your allegiance, and I'm telling you all of this for your own good. You've got to watch your step at all times. We live in a fishbowl in this business, and even a golden wonder like you can drown himself if he ain't careful. You want to get ahead in this man's outfit — and I think you do, you're the type, and I've studied your record — then you can't go off swimming against the current. Get yourself in hot water, Georgie-boy, and your ass is cooked."

I'd heard that JFK actually wanted to retire Hoover, but the Old Man had accumulated so much dirt about the president's personal lifestyle, all secreted in the director's infamous file, that Kennedy was unable to fire or retire him without devastating public revelations about his own incessant sexual exploits. Jack's licentious behavior was widely known, but in that day the media was still a tame watchdog, and there were no tabloids or Internet sources to exploit such rancid personal behavior.

JFK and Hoover had apparently come to a mutual live-and-let-live relationship. Hoover's relationship with brother Robert, however, was full of ill-concealed mutual hatred. And for Hoover, to be administratively beholden to such youthful arrogance was almost more than the old man could take. They were at each other's throats, behind each other's backs, 24-hours a day.

FBI agents, therefore, walked a fine line. We worked for J. Edgar Hoover, but the director of the FBI officially worked for the attorney general, Robert Kennedy. For both men, and for us, it was an intolerable condition. I'd sensed an impasse building that would soon require everyone in the Bureau to choose sides. It would have been unthinkable in the past; Hoover's word had been uncontested for thirty-eight years. But it was Bobby and Jack now, and blood was thicker than administrative longevity

"Aw, the hell with this," Gene said with genuine irritation. "I gotta go eat."

"Hold it, Gene. Give me another minute, please. I understand what you're saying, but don't you ever question him?"

He zipped up his jacket, chewing on the as-yet un-lighted cigar. "I told you before, kid, I do my job, and then I go eat and grab some sleep before starting all over again. I'm proud to be an FBI agent, see, proud of the Bureau and what it stands for, and I'm damn proud of the director. In my book he's one of the greatest Americans in our history. There've been a lot of presidents, and attorneys general come and go. Only been one J. Edgar Hoover, and there'll never be another."

I would be more circumspect from now on. One word from Gene in the right, or wrong place, and I would be a former agent of the FBI.

When he was gone, I secured the door bolt and angrily placed the headset above my ears. But who was I mad at — Gene, Mr. Hoover, the Kennedys, or myself? Maybe I was just envious of Gene Elliott's simple loyalties.

What — or who — was *I* willing to kill for?

I tried to settle down to the night's work. I should have been listening to the mike talk in case something significant developed, but I couldn't stop my roiling thoughts. All my life, as a boy during World War II, I'd fantasized about becoming a G-man and combating Nazis and other anti-American evil-doers. Then what the hell was the matter with me now? Why was I so conflicted?

What I thought I knew that others — even Hoover and his G-men — didn't seem to know was because of the special circumstances of my life. Lately I'd developed a sour intimation in the pit of my stomach about where all of this was heading.

Gene was my friend, but I had also been befriended by Fred Osborn, a ranking suit up in the Springfield field office, who in effect ran it all. The Special Agent in Charge (SAC) was reputed to be little more than a front man, a Hoover crony of slight talent.

Fred, however, was the real deal. He'd worked his way up the ladder over the years and, for some reason, had taken a special interest in me. He still liked to work the field on occasion and had, just before this present undercover assignment in East St. Louis, chosen me to partner with him on a fugitive surveillance job. We spent most of one night together in an abandoned railroad car while keeping watch on the target house across the tracks. The culprit didn't show up on our watch — we got him a week later — so it gave us a lot of time to talk. Even to this day I remember the gist of our conversation.

"How was SOG?" I asked and passed him a cup of thermos coffee.

He shuddered and said, "God, it's so good to be back in the boonies. Too much time with the suits and ... well, you'll find out in due course. I managed to avoid the director's wrath, though. So it wasn't all bad."

"Is he really as eccentric as some say or ..."

"More than you can imagine. And you'll find out about that, too. There's no escaping his reach."

FBI agents were totally at the mercy of the personal whims of the director. The Hoover Cult had been in force for more than thirty years. He required agents to put in two or three unpaid overtime hours daily and to be on call twenty-four hours a day every day. There was no real family life, especially during undercover assignments, as I now had good reason to know.

Here's how it worked: No matter where you might go in the evening after the day's duty — dinner in a restaurant, a football game, or a movie — you had to call in to the office beforehand and report your destination and how long you would be there. Hoover would randomly select an agent in the field, call for him, and if contact was not immediately forthcoming, the agent was censored. Censure could include a fine, demotion, or an overnight transfer from one side of the country to the other. A second violation most often meant dismissal with prejudice, which meant that you could never thereafter aspire to another government job.

"Times are tough right now," Fred said. "The president is treading hot water. He's had so damned many problems in so short a time. Ike and Nixon launched so many off-the-book adventures that are coming home to roost. The Bay of Pigs fiasco almost did Jack in before he got his rocking chair grooved. And now with his talk of withdrawing combat forces from Vietnam, he's alienated the old guard at the Company as well as the Joint Chiefs."

It was the first I'd heard of such Vietnam talk, and I was all ears. I loved this kind of insider information and hunched forward over the scraps of our cold supper. But it wasn't necessary to urge Fred on; tonight he was wired. It was good that we had another agent under the boxcar, since we weren't paying attention to the target house across the tracks. "Look, I know you're wondering why I'm talking to you like this. This sort of thing isn't often done in the Bureau. But your case is special. That's why I've taken such an interest."

Special? What did he mean by that?

"I've studied your background in some detail. All-American-boy type — no, don't laugh. Smart, athletic, good lower middle-class upbringing. Only child. Born and raised Protestant, schooled in Catholic institutions — high school and college — by the Jesuits."

I didn't know what to say, so I said nothing.

"Star athlete in high school down there in Tampa, basketball scholarship to college over in New Orleans. Excellent military record — top-secret security work involving hush-hush activities in Texas and New Mexico and across the border in Mexico. After law school you could have gone any way you chose — private practice, military intelligence, CIA, FBI. You joined the Bureau, attracted attention in training school, and now you're on your way to becoming one of Hoover's fair-haired boys."

"Whoa! He doesn't even know I'm alive."

"The director knows fucking all," he said with a sour smile.

I shut up and waited him out. I knew there was more to come. "You were assigned all the case work of a new agent. Edgar especially appreciated the way you rooted out that Commie professor down-state. And you done real good on that bank robbery case outside Springfield, and your work on the kidnap/murder case of the local judge's teenage daughter."

Mention of the latter case made my flesh crawl. It was a typical kidnap for ransom; only the bastard had mailed a sample of the girl's golden pubic hair to the judge to prove that she was in captivity.

"When you guys tracked down the girl's body sunk in that abandoned well ..."

He drained his coffee and said, "Okay, now let me finish. All these things are true and valuable, no doubt about it. But best of all, George, you have a coterie of friends — the kind of friends that matter."

I was so uneasy now I was about to piss in my pants.

"And I'm not just blowing smoke. Here, take a look." He shoved a hand inside his coat pocket, and I hoped to hell that he wasn't reaching for an un-traceable piece with which to silence me permanently. But he withdrew a small packet and passed it over. In it were two black-and-white photographs. I felt as if Fred had nailed me to the carriage wall.

****

The grind continued day and night in defense of our country. The mikes were seldom silent, and we recorded it all. And soon I'd come to recognize most of their voices and often mingled with some of the wiseguys up close and personal for lunch or coffee. I wore loafers, slacks and a casual jacket rather than the customary FBI attire of three-piece suit and snap-brim hat. But we had to get out and about; we couldn't look like we were in hiding. Of course that's exactly what we were doing, hiding, but in plain sight. I disliked that part of the job, getting to know some of the guys and even going so far as to make them like me. But it was all part of the job.

"Fuckin' swamp rats. Don' talk no better English dan da fuckin' Cubans."

"Cajun friends of Marcello workin' wit' da exiles down in the bayous dere."

It was a strange sensation, disturbing, to eavesdrop on conversations about people and places that I was personally familiar with. In my college days in New Orleans, I'd often seen and talked with Carlos Marcello around the mob's French Quarter hangouts, most of which he owned. He was boss of the controlling crime family that encompassed not only New Orleans, but territory extending north into Mississippi and Arkansas, and westward into Texas as far as Dallas.

Fred had said that Marcello might well be the most powerful don in the country The sign that he kept posted on the office door of his New Orleans headquarters in the Town and Country Motel and Restaurant complex read: THREE CAN KEEP A SECRET/WHEN TWO ARE DEAD.

One day at lunch, a pair of wiseguys in the booth next to me were running their mouths in the daily effort to give the appearance of being big-shots in the know.

"Trouble is, ya can't trust people t'do the right thing no more. This kid, Bobby, rat-bastard. Look what he's tryin' to do to Marcello. Deportation, IRS harassment, phony indictments. An' Momo, he can't take a leak up dere in Chi wit'out a fuckin' Feebie lookin' down his pants. Probably got color prints of Momo shoving it to the pres's girlfriend. Next ya know there'll be a pack of Feebies down here harassing our crew. Fuckin' Bobby's got awl the goddamned G-guys with hards-on all of a sudden."

"All except da Hoov," his table mate said, "J. Edna can't get no hard-on."

I made a mental note of the raucous laughter and indistinguishable comments that followed this exchange but hadn't the slightest idea what do with it. I sure couldn't include it in an official report to the file. Hoover would probably fire me just for having listened to such personal filth that in any way involved him.

"Our people been workin' wit Hoov for years," said the first guy. "An accommodation, ya know what I mean?"

"Yeah, goddamn brudders causin' awl da trouble."

"Snot-nosed pricks, 'specially da kid brudder, dere."

"Mean liddle cocksucker, like his old man. Get his he ain't careful, y'know what I mean?"

"Blow his fuckin' head off!"

You couldn't tell when this stuff was anything more than infantile wiseguy posturing and tribal braggadocio, but you couldn't take a chance of overlooking anything significant. I would at least make notes of the slurs against Mr. Hoover's character and the potential danger to the Kennedy brothers when I got back to the office.

"Talk is da boss is all cut up about da request from da man in Chi."

"Yeah, say dey got trouble in Florida wit da man down dere."

I tensed up at the mention of a possible connection between these guys and the Trafficante family in Florida. We had a pretty good idea what was going on with the government connections with Marcello and the exile communities in New Orleans and down in Miami. Off the books, the Company was said to be teaming up with elements of the Mafia to assassinate Cuba's Fidel Castro.

The covert operators at CIA — the old guard from World War II's OSS brigands who had all moved over in lock-step to the new agency — figured there was no one better to pull off such a hit than the Mafia. Why not conspire with them under good cover and get rid of a common enemy?

I was so keyed up I could hardly eat my lunch. If only these guys would linger over dessert. I knew the mob had good reason to cooperate, even with the hated government. They hated Castro more for closing down their moneymaking playpen in Havana. Rumor reaching us — a lot of this came to me by way of my special relationship with Fred Osborn — was that a lot of money had been paid to the mob, and the Company was eager for results. But now, according to these two turkeys, the question seemed to be if Santo Trafficante, the boss in Florida and the former king-pin in Havana before Castro, was dragging his feet. Or was there something else involved?

Carlos Marcello

"What I hear is da man in Chi is some pissed. Maybe even da whol' Commissione. Somethin' gotta be done, dey say."

This had me sitting up straight with my mouth wide open. Was Santo in trouble with some of his own people? I wanted to talk with Fred in the worst kind of way. But I had a sudden premonition that it might be better for me to simply finish lunch, get the hell out of here and talk about this with no one. Of course, I failed to take my own counsel and immediately arranged a private conference with Fred Osborn.

We had coffee one night in a safe café on the river near Dupo. I was learning firsthand just how much the Bureau and the Mafia had in common. Life in both outfits was like a love affair: you lived in a state of high-anxiety at all times. Who did what? Who said what? Why did you call? Why didn't you call? Where are you going? Where have you been? You're early; you're late. Why? Why? Why?

"You did the right thing, now calm down." He stirred sugar into his coffee and said, "Look, I don't know everything myself. But as far as I can tell, the Bureau's not involved. It's CIA — at least the covert thugs who run these things for the Company — working with their cronies in the mob. *Some* of the mobsters, mind you, not everybody."

I held my breath. I thought this was the moment for him to say something about the two photos he had shown me the other night, photos of Santo Trafficante and Carlos Marcello, two of the most powerful Mafia dons in the country, both of whom I was acquainted with. But Fred was silent for a long moment, and I supposed he was making up his mind about how far he should go with this.

"Here's the working premise," he finally said. "The mob helps get rid of Castro. That gives cover for the government, total denial, and in return the A.G.'s office will cut back on its harassment of the mob, including Marcello. Everybody wins. The Company will pay, the mob will play. A lot of money has already passed over. Feverish arrangements are being made with a pack of *agents provocateurs* in New Orleans — some of those guys you paled around with in your college days — and others down in Miami."

We weren't *pals,* I wanted to say but didn't. I wanted to know about Santo.

"Okay, now what I hear is that Trafficante's pulling a fast one. He's taking the money, but he's not serious about the venture at all. It's a sham on his part. Makes it look like he's on board but he has no intention of completing the job." Fred paused again and then nailed me. "There's even talk that he's playing both sides of the street; that he's actually working with Castro."

"Aw, c'mon, Fred, no. That's bullshit. Got to be."

"After the takeover in Cuba in '58, all the mobsters were banished from Havana, all except Santo. Story has it that an arrangement was made with Fidel. Santo would provide the U.S. pipeline for the burgeoning drug trade that would run through Cuba, and they would split the take."

I probably knew more about this than Fred and the government. After the takeover, Fidel finally had Santo arrested. But was the arrest a bogus front for their accommodation? I'd known the lawyer who went down to handle Santo's case for most of my life, and two of my oldest friends eventually became his law partners in Tampa. In due course, Santo was released and returned home. Was the whole thing a sham?

"So, to a lot of people it all looks phony," Fred said.

"Mr. Hoover included?"

A brief pause followed the mention of the man's name. It was suddenly as if he was at the table with us.

"As far as I know, the director's not involved in any way," Fred finally said. "It's not even clear if the new CIA director knows what's going on. Dulles would have been on top of things, of course, but after the Bay of Pigs fiasco he had to go. JFK blamed him for the whole debacle."

Then he laughed, really laughed. "Now I got this first-hand from a man in the know. Jack said that 'CIA estimates weren't worth dog shit,' his actual phrase. After his reelection, he really seems determined to shut them down and spread their responsibilities around the wheel. They say it's bad now with very little communication between Langley and the White House, and it's going to get worse. Kennedy really means to make them pay."

"Can he get away with it, actually shut them down?"

"The sixty-four-dollar question in all of this brouhaha." We went outside and sat in Fred's car. "You see how crazy it is. JFK's obsessed with Cuba, and Bobby's got the rag on for the Mafia. One minute they're telling the Company they mean to destroy them, the next demanding their help. And they want help from the mob too, but Bobby won't lay off his pet targets, Marcello and Giancana. A witch's brew is being ..."

"Jesus!" I suddenly exploded, "maybe the Kennedys don't know what the Company's up to! Maybe they don't *know* that a deal has been made with the Mafia to whack Fidel even while Bobby is still determined to wipe the mob out."

Fred looked at me in the shadows as if I had just rung the bell, and I didn't have the balls to inquire for whom it might be tolling.

It was after 3 a.m. and I had yet to go to bed. I was a wreck. What to do? I didn't dare turn on the alcohol tap, so I took a glass of warm milk to the only comfortable chair in my one-room bedsitter. But I was anything but comfortable and felt the milk curdle on my stomach. I'd never counted on anything like this and had no experience or training to fall back on. I'd always imagined that things would be black or white, right or wrong, once I joined the Bureau. But now ...

I went over to the window and looked down on the street below. It was dark and deserted. The rain had stopped, but storm clouds still hovered in the vicinity. I wondered what the weather was like down in Tampa.

Was the president in danger? Bobby, too? And just what kind of trouble was Santo in and from how many directions? But the real question in my mind was what I was going to do about it?

My lungs filled with congested air. My relationship with the Mafia started in Tampa in 1945. I was eleven years old and looked it, a blue-eyed towhead wearing a T-shirt and shorts, with knobby knees and scruffy sneakers. All during the war I'd sold war bonds, collected old newspapers, bottles and scrap metal for the war effort.

I was pulling my empty wagon on my return trip from the junkyard over by Ross Avenue with twenty dollars cash in my pocket. A man in sweaty khakis said he'd show me his "thing" if I would show him mine.

"I'll even give ya a dollar, whataya say, kid?"

I said, "I gotta go home," and my response seemed to make him mad.

"Well, shitmaroo, buddy-boy, how much ya think your liddle pecker's worth?"

He grabbed my shoulder in a way that made my flesh crawl. What did he want?

Was he drunk, crazy, or what? Lord, I couldn't tell Mama about any of this, she'd never let me go out alone again. But when I tried to move on along the sidewalk, the man became more insistent. He blocked the wagon with his foot and increased the pressure on my neck and shoulder. There was something wild in his expression.

"You better leave me alone," I said in a wavering voice.

Cars passed in both directions on nearby Tampa Street, and an approaching streetcar rattled, but no one was paying any attention to us.

"Where you been with that wagon? I bet you a real enterprisin' liddle patriot, ain't you? Been sellin' scrap metal for us soljur-boys, hey?" I tugged away from him but tripped on the wagon tongue, and before I could get up, the man was all over me. "Liddle bastard. Take your money an' your dick an' make you like it. I'll …"

But he was suddenly head-over-heels and rolling in the dirt and sandspurs next to me. Another man pounded the soldier with hammer-like blows from his fists, which were fitted with brass fixtures. Somehow, the soldier broke loose and staggered to his feet, his nose spouting blood. He threw a handful of dirt into his assailant's eyes and ran away as fast as his wobbly legs would carry him.

I stood panting as the man brushed sand out of his face and hair and then said, "You okay there, kid?"

"Oh, yeah," I stammered. "I mean, yessir. Thanks for your help."

"Don't mention it," he said with a graceful flick of his hand.

I'd seen him many times around the neighborhood, but never up this close and personal. He spoke good English, only slightly accented. He wasn't tall and was dressed nice, like a businessman. His hair was lightish-brown and he had eyes like none I'd ever seen: green. They shone in the night like moonlight on the phosphorous water over in the nearby Gulf. He picked up his panama hat, brushed it, and put it on with a snappy flourish. Then he gestured over his shoulder to an old four-door Chevy parked at the curb with the driver's door standing open. "Guy won't bother you no more, but maybe I should give you a ride home."

"I'm okay. I don't live far from here, over by the playground."

He peered at me closely in the waning light. "I thought you looked familiar. I see a game every now and then. Remember, see the ball, hit the ball."

"I sure will, Mr. ..."

"Trafficante," he said.

"Yes, sir. I deliver newspapers to your father."

"Likes his paper flat, not rolled."

"He told me so the first day."

He laughed and gave me another wave of his hand and then started for his car.

"Mr. Trafficante," I called out, "thanks again for your help."

He looked over his shoulder and said, "Forget about it, kid. That's what friends are for."

I watched as my new friend drove away, righted my wagon, and then turned toward home and my future.

PART TWO

Ties that Bind

In Illinois, after I heard my childhood acquaintance, Santo Trafficante, was in danger, I spent a sleepless night. What should I do? I was a member of the FBI and I was also a friend. Rain hammered down when I started for the office the next morning. I stopped at a phone booth. A gust of cold wind buffeted the booth as I tried to keep my voice under control. "No, I can't give you my name. Tell him I said he never could hit a slider low on the inside."

Moments later a voice from the past was on the line. "Okay, cracker. You sure know how to snag a guy's attention."

"This has to be fast and confidential. No names. Get me a number close by."

I couldn't risk talking to him on his office phone in case his line was being tapped. He gave me the number of a phone booth one block from his law office and answered my call on the first ring. We'd known each other since childhood. Before I'd left for the Bureau training school, he'd offered to hook up with me as soon as I came to my senses and decided to hang out my shingle. Now, in fewer than twenty words I told him that one of his best clients might soon expect to have serious trouble and why.

"Conjo!" he exclaimed in a shocked whisper. "How can I contact you?"

"You can't, ever."

"We owe you, *amigo.*"

"Forget you ever *heard* of me!"

In Tampa, my mother and I lived together in a boarding house in a working-class neighborhood — "Joined at the hip," other roomers said — and spent every waking hour together. We went for long walks beside the river and in nearby grassy parks, movies two and three times a week, and church on Sunday. Mama was not particularly religious, but it was the thing to do in those days. One week Baptist, the next Methodist. She never held a job, and I have no idea where our money for living expenses came from. I was happy.

Then John Mettler suddenly appeared when I was five years old, and we moved to a single-family dwelling nearby. No two people could have been more mismatched for marriage. While my beautiful mother was blonde and high-school educated, John

33

was a semi-literate runt with reddish hair who referred to me as "Boy" until the day he died.

During all the time after John came into our lives, Mama remained a conventional stay-at-home wife and mother. She kept our little house spotlessly clean, our clothes washed and ironed, and her flower beds were the talk of the neighborhood. She grew fruits and vegetables in the back yard. Meanwhile, John worked alternately as a carpenter, shipbuilder and brewery salesman. Eventually, he became a branch manager of the brewery that was said to be owned by the local Mafia. In those days I had no idea what a mafia was. Even during the height of the Depression, John was apparently able to utilize his talents and varied contacts to make ends meet. But he was never a father to me.

I spent hours holed up in my room with my radio, newspapers, books and magazines in an effort to understand what was happening in our world. Even at that early age, I was a newshound. In 1938, a Boston millionaire named Joseph P. Kennedy was appointed as America's ambassador to the Court of St. James and moved his family to London with the intention of keeping America out of war. Kennedy had already sent one of his sons, John F. Kennedy, on a tour of Europe, and I remember wishing that I had a father who was so good to me. Jack, as the boy was called, was a sickly child, and his tour was interrupted when he fell ill in Germany and had to rejoin his family for the London assignment.

By 1940, Hitler and his German army had begun absorbing other neighboring countries, and it looked as if he had no intention of stopping. Also, a bunch called the Loyalists had recently surrendered to a Hitler clone named Franco down in Spain, and I really had no idea what *that* was all about. In the weeks and months following the Japanese attack on our Naval base in Hawaii, a national draft law had been passed by Congress, and ration books and tokens for food, bus and streetcar transportation became mandatory. Gasoline for cars became hard to come by. John, a WWI veteran, was too old for military service but managed well enough as a carpenter at the Tampa shipyards throughout the war, and to do *my* duty as a good citizen, I signed up for a morning newspaper route.

My number-one hero during the early war years was J. Edgar Hoover and his courageous G-men. I read all the FBI comic books that I could lay my hands on and never missed a radio episode of "FBI in Peace and War." I just hoped the war wouldn't end before I could become a heroic G-man myself, a spy-catcher extraordinaire. And before sleep each night, I pretended my real father was none other than J. Edgar Hoover.

I was just a kid in a world in which it behooved children to grow up as fast as they could. I spent most nights alone in my room behind closed doors with my map and radio, my books and magazines, and my extensive collection of comic books. Only The Shadow and I knew what evil lurked in the hearts of men.

In 1942, we received a distinguished visitor at 108 W. Warren. I'd just turned eight years old and was walking home from the playground when I saw the military sedan with a soldier in uniform standing guard. I bounded up the front stairs sans military bearing, and Mama called out through the screen door, "Oh, hi, Sonny, come meet your Uncle Charles."

He was real, he truly did exist. He was not a big man but *seemed* big. He was neat, trim and wore his uniform like it had been molded on him, and there were four rows of beautiful ribbons and badges on his chest and a pair of wonderful gold chicken bars on his shoulders.

Colonel Charles G. Mettler! Protector of men, women and defenseless children, and the stalwart guardian of our nation at war. Was I impressed? It might just as well have been General Eisenhower.

Uncle Charles had come and gone before news reports revealed what he was doing in Florida. A number of Nazi U-boat saboteurs had been captured off the Atlantic coastline in Long Island and Florida. The military intelligence officer in charge of the Florida capture was Colonel Charles G. Mettler.

If John was home during his brother's visit, he stayed in his room.

I later learned that while German submarines were operating off the east coast of the United States, there had been numerous acts of sabotage on the docks in New York harbor. Docks that, of course, were mob controlled.

At that time the mob was presided over by one Lucky Luciano as the chairman of the syndicate's National Commission. Luciano, however, was conducting his affairs from his Dannemora prison cell, having been sentenced to a long term on a prostitution conviction. The U.S. Navy offered a deal to the wily crime lord: transfer to a country club federal prison in return for dock security. The bargain was struck. Luciano was duly transferred to a luxurious confinement, and there were no more acts of sabotage in the New York harbor.

And still again in 1943, Luciano's aid was sought in connection with the Allied invasion of Sicily. He sent instructions to the mob in his homeland to cooperate with the Allies. They did so and the invasion was accomplished with considerable finesse as a direct result of such assistance.

After the war, U.S. rewards to the Sicilian Mafia made it a greater power in that country than it had ever been. Luciano was released from prison but exiled to Italy and never allowed to return to America. He continued to operate as the head of the worldwide organized crime apparatus, however, until his death by heart attack in Rome in 1962.

As war and life moved into 1943, another part of my home escape routine was roaming about the city streets on bicycle, skates and/or shanks

Lucky Luciano

mare, and any means by which I could avoid my mother's unrelenting scrutiny. I was still reading and listening to my radio, and before winter came that year news reached us out of Pacific waters of the heroic deeds of a young PT-boat commander who, although wounded, managed to rescue his entire crew when his boat was sunk by enemy attack. He was called Jack, and that was about all that I knew about him in that day. But I would have cause in later life to fill in the gaps.

In those days the Tampa Bay area was known in the media as "The Hell-Hole of the Gulf Coast." Had the famed Russian writer set one of his stories in Tampa, Dostoevsky may well have entitled his world-famous book *Crime and* Selective *Punishment.*

Tampa at that time was one of the most corrupt environments in the country. Of course this is hindsight on my part. I had no understanding of such matters during my youth, just as the vast majority of citizens today have little or no idea of the endemic corruption that still infects our cities and states, as well as extensive elements of our federal government.

The Trafficantes, however, flew pretty much under the national radar, and it was not until the Kefauver Senate racket hearings in the early 1950s that the name acquired a degree of national prominence. I was still pretty wet behind the ears, but by the time I'd left middle school in the late '40s, there had been some fifty unsolved murders in Tampa involving internal power struggles for control of syndicate operations throughout the southern states and Cuba. Many of these deaths involved family members of my friends and schoolmates and all such conflict always ended with the strengthening of the Trafficante grip on syndicate operations.

The advent of Prohibition back in 1920 had catapulted every small-time racketeer throughout the country into contested territory for wealth and power on a scale never before imagined on this side of the ocean.

Do you remember the PT-109 incident during the war and the heroic young naval officer named John F. Kennedy? Well his wealthy father, Joseph P. Kennedy Sr. was in the decade of the '20s on the road to multi-millions of surplus dollars gained from his personal involvement in the trafficking of illegal liquor. His cohorts were people like Frank Costello of New York and numerous other powerful Mafiosi who catered to protected speakeasies and society's wealthy aristocracy. A scarlet reputation as a bootlegger, mob entrepreneur and busy womanizer would cling to Kennedy Sr. for the rest of his life and cause no end of trouble and shame for his family.

But no amount of money could buy health and happiness for his children. His son Jack had been stricken with scarlet fever at an early age and would remain a sickly boy and man all of his life. His daughter Rosemary was diagnosed as mentally retarded and was institutionalized. During those tumultuous days Joe Sr. moved into the movie business, made millions, and commenced a long relationship with actress Gloria Swanson. It was an openly illicit affair, one of many, and his long-suffering wife Rose was powerless to respond since, as a devout Catholic, divorce was not an option.

As the decade of the '30s dawned, the Tampa Bay area entered what came to be known as the "Era of Blood." During this period Santo Trafficante Sr. became the undisputed boss of the Tampa syndicate. His is a story ripped from the pages of an unpublished Mario Puzo manuscript. He was born in 1914 in Sicily, immigrated to America at sixteen, and became a naturalized citizen in 1925. By this time he had established a family of five sons and a reputation as an up-and-coming leader in the Tampa Mafia, and the jewel in his crown was thought to be Cuba.

But again I'm speaking of things here that I did not yet know about, that I certainly did not comprehend. What I had come to understand, however, was that personal mistakes often carried dire penalties and little in the way of forgiveness. And soon my newspaper route became a burden and, to my mother's great relief, I gave it up.

My decision came about in this way

I think I had recently turned twelve years old. I know it happened on a Saturday summer morning when I was on the streets dutifully collecting from my regular subscribers. I was met by an open door at a house no more than a mile from my own and, upon knocking, was instructed to come on in, that my money was waiting. I followed the voice through another open door into a bathroom where the lady of the house waited in all her naked splendor in a tub of sudsy water.

What followed on this occasion and two succeeding Saturday mornings would certainly in this day be labeled child abuse, but I labeled her front door "The Gates of Paradise." However, when I proudly revealed this new relationship to my best friend, he reacted with alarm rather than the lascivious envy that I'd expected.

"Good God Almighty, you asshole! Don't you *know* who her keeper is?"

And he told me.

Well I'd never heard the phrase "a made man," or the title "wiseguy," nor would I have known what to make of them at that time had I done so. And the word *goomada* — mistress — meant nothing to me. But having now made the discovery of just *how* this "made woman's" ambitious keeper was employed, and by whom, I had sense enough to know that this phase of newspapering was over for me. I turned in my collection book, drew a few dollars back pay and "retired" from active duty.

Ironically, I would become a journalism major in college and would co-own and operate two weekly newspapers in the distant future. I always figured that I had learned the nuts and bolts of the profession from the bottom up.

One summer afternoon in 1949 — I was about fourteen and had just completed junior high school — I rode home on my bicycle after hours of invigorating baseball at nearby Plymouth Playground and came upon the most astounding sight. In our living room on Warren Avenue sat my mother and a distinguished looking man wearing a long black dress.

In spite of the heat, Mama wore her best flowered chintz that she usually saved for church occasions. She looked gorgeous so blonde, slender and mysterious. The man with her wore a starched white collar high up around his neck and a sash tied around his waist. He was tall with jet black hair parted near the middle and a friendly smile that I would come to look for every morning for the next four years.

"Oh, there you are," Mama said excitedly. "Come in and meet Father Hargrove."

"Hello, young man." The priest put out his hand and said, "I've been looking forward to meeting you. I've heard so many good things about you."

Mama was fair to bursting with pride and I said, "You've heard about me?"

"I have indeed," he smiled.

It seems that the priest had come to make my family an offer that we could not refuse.

A Made Man

PART THREE

Hell-Hole of the Gulf Coast

As we know a time did come in later life when I became a bona fide member of the G-man team. Let me say up front, however, that it was not always a time of glory and personal heroism such as was imagined by that little boy during his nighttime escape fantasies at 108 W. Warren in Tampa.

"Jesus, George, how did you get a foot in the door, let alone emerge with a badge and credentials?"

"What do you mean by that?" I asked Ron Hinchley with bogus naïveté over a plate of river catfish the size of my shoes. I was at HQ in Springfield for the weekend for a round of administrative paper shuffling. It had been my first field assignment after training school in 1961. My first wife Pattie and I had maintained an apartment here after my transfer to the Resident Agency in Carbondale, and we also set up a small apartment down there. But most of my time was spent elsewhere on undercover assignment. Pattie and I had married in 1958 in a military crossed swords ceremony, but we had seen very little of each other in recent months.

Agents assigned to undercover missions were rotated back to headquarters periodically for administrative duties and firearms requalification. We had to account for what we were doing and the suits scrutinized our reported activities for any discrepancies. I'd learned early-on in the Bureau that someone was always looking over my shoulder.

I knew what Ron was getting at but wasn't going to make it easy for him. I stirred my coffee and watched the passing parade outside the window. It was high noon on a cold, beautiful day. You could see the Illinois state capitol building across the way and I wondered where Honest Abe had eaten lunch during his noon breaks from his courtroom labors. When I was a kid, he'd been one of my special heroes and here I was in his hometown with Lincoln memorabilia all around me.

Recently I'd even been offered an association with a prominent law firm in Springfield, in spite of my non-residency. Just think, I would try cases in the same courtroom in which Lincoln had honed his craft. Needless to say, I was tempted. I wasn't at all sure how much longer I could take the cramped FBI lifestyle. It wasn't anything like what I'd expected, and I wasn't cut out for it. But what was I going to do about it?

"You know damned well what I'm talking about," Ron said. "Remember, I'm a G-man, too, a certified member of the greatest law enforcement agency in the history of the world. Amen. Nothing escapes my attention." He affected a Sherlock Holmes looking-glass posture, examined the menu for dessert, and we both cracked up.

Ron had been with the Bureau for sixteen months and was unlikely to make it through twenty-four. He said he'd almost rejected the credentials after he completed new agents training at Quantico. I accused him of being the recruit we'd heard about who'd shot the nuts off the John Wayne mock-up during the quick-draw exercise.

"How long can *you* stand all of this cloak-and-dagger horseshit, even if they let you stay around?" he asked. "Look what happened to Barney."

Barney McCall was an old hand who had mentored us both in turn upon our arrivals in Springfield. He was a super-fine agent who got the job done. Unfortunately, he'd also done the job with the wife of a county commissioner and was dismissed from the Bureau with prejudice, all within a few hours of the discovery.

"Eight good years down the drain over a piece of ass," Ron groused.

Agents were all of a piece as far as the director was concerned. Any agent could be replaced by another without a moment's slow-down in the work process. Wives, children and sweethearts were expected to toe the mark. The primary rule for agents and their families was to never embarrass the Bureau. Break the rule and suffer the consequence.

Unless working undercover, agents were required to wear suits and ties in the office at all times and hats when working outside the office. No facial hair, no bushy sideburns. In the office no coffee, tea or snacks could be consumed. You had an hour for lunch and woe betides any agent who was late signing in on the return sheet.

I wasn't keen about pursuing this conversation, but Ron wasn't about to let up. "Look, I overheard super Wilson talking about you last week with one of his assistants. When they saw me, they clammed up. But it looks like they may have you in their sights. Something was said about controversial contacts in your early years that somehow weren't turned up in your background investigation."

"That's bullshit, Ron. You know those guys, always looking for an opportunity to kiss ass with the SAC, hoping he'll put in a good word with the fat guy in the three-piece suit at SOG."

By now I knew exactly how the Bureau operated and how administrative promotion was attained. There were two primary groupings — field agents and administrative hacks. Field agents were the heart and soul of the G-man force, but the suits had the upper hand. A fine agent's career could be ruined in a skinny minute by their malicious handiwork, all performed under the FBI banner of Fidelity, Bravery and Integrity. I'm told the Bureau doesn't operate in this horse-and-buggy manner today and hope the stories are true.

"Okay, I understand if you don't want to talk about it. But watch your back, buddy-boy. The suits *are* talking." He signaled to the waitress for our checks.

Controversial contacts, Ron had said. Well, let me tell you about some of that.

It was entirely through an accident of birth that I'd lived as a child in the same neighborhood as Santo Trafficante Sr., who was alleged to control organized crime activities in Florida and a portion of the Southeast and who was said to practically *own* Cuba in those pre-Castro days of rampant corruption and licentiousness. And he was reputed to enjoy close working associations with the other leading mobsters of the day, such as Lucky Luciano and Meyer Lansky from New York, Anthony Accardo from Chicago, and Mickey Cohen from Los Angeles.

I grew up in the long shadow of his son, Santo Jr., my benefactor on the street that eventful night at war's end. He would become head of the Tampa "family" when his father died from heart failure in 1954 and would retain this dominant position until his own death by natural causes in 1987. By that time he was alleged in many circles to have been complicit in the assassination of President Kennedy.

I knew many of the family members and business associates, including Santo Jr.'s daughters and a nephew, Santo Trafficante III, who was my younger schoolmate from high school days.

I was not intimate with the Trafficante family and its enterprise. I knew many family members and they knew me, but to my knowledge I never worked for them. Although in truth, such a fine line cannot be drawn with respect to my law practice that developed for a short time in the mid-sixties after President Kennedy's death and my FBI service. But I have never in any way knowingly represented any of the "family" business.

Although a number of my childhood friends grew up to become mob lawyers, the appellation never applied to me. One friend, the nephew of a murdered family capo, was later elected to two effective terms as our local Hillsborough County State's Attorney. Two other friends in due course came to represent Santo Jr., Carlos Marcello, and Teamster boss Jimmy Hoffa.

In the late '40s and '50s, the Tampa Bay region was a magnate for such conspicuous figures of JFK assassination lore as David Ferrie, a homosexual New Orleans soldier-of-fortune of scandalous reputation, and Jack Ruby, a psychotic arms dealer down from Chicago who operated with Trafficante family permission in Tampa and Havana before and during WWII. Later, Ruby returned South, along with Ferrie and others, to run guns to Batista *and* to Castro, again with Santo Jr.'s permission. I knew both men during my college days in New Orleans, and both of them wound up in the service of mob interests in Dallas, Texas in 1963.

David Ferrie

Ferrie looked me up — I was in my last year of law school — to see if I might be willing to assist in the cause that was boiling in the Caribbean. I realize now that the Mafia *and* the CIA were both hedging their bets as to which side would emerge victorious in Cuba, an environment that they continued to view as their private playpen. Ferrie had intimated that through my wife Pattie's birth connections in the Cayman Islands, I could develop relationships that would greatly benefit the cause. I had no such interests and turned him down flat.

One of my closest childhood friends and high school classmates was Philip Agee, who would become the notorious CIA turncoat of the seventies and beyond. He lived the last decades of his life in exile with a price on his head anywhere in which he could find temporary sanctuary. My life might have developed along the lines of Phil's had I not chosen to pass through another door into the world of developing manhood.

We met for hamburgers and milk shakes one day shortly before our graduation from high school in 1952. "We're not supposed to talk about it," he said.

"I won't rat you out, if you won't tell on me. But from your descriptions, I'm pretty sure it's the same guy."

We knew our mysterious enigmatic recruiter only as Martin, clearly a bogus operational name that he pronounced "Marteen." I would soon come to know how the CIA worked, at least in its covert operations, with everything and everybody off the books. No one knew exactly whom or what they were working for, or whom they were working with. You could share a desk with another case officer for years and not know him or her by a true name.

I never got a handle on Martin, and he was replaced at varying intervals by other recruiters, but he always popped up again at unpropitious moments and gave the impression that he had been watching all along. He was a moderately tall, slender man with thinning blond hair, pale sunburned skin and fiery blue eyes. A compulsive drinker, he gave one the impression of harboring a homosexual bent. I don't know about Phil, but I would often run across him in the coming years, a few times in Mexico City, often in and around the Caribbean basin, and once in London. We always met in dicey situations, and he was always using shifting aliases and a variety of disguises.

"I think he's been working on a couple other guys at school, too."

I spooned up some ice cream. "Are *you* listening to him?"

"I think so. Graduation from college, three years in the Air Force as cover, and then ..." He fell into a deep thoughtful silence. I knew he had another CIA contact, a friend of his father who worked in Washington, D.C., but he never used her name with me. Although we were good friends, there was a lot about Phil that I never got to know, and vice versa, which is the way it should have been.

"What the hell do CIA agents do anyway?" I asked. "I mean really *do*?"

Neither of us had any good answers back in that day. I've always wondered how our lives would have worked out had we just said no when dubious opportunity came knocking. But that last summer before college was hectic and unsettling to me in many ways. What did I really want to do?

I wanted to write books. But I couldn't say it to anyone. I still lacked the inner surety to make such a dream known to others. In any case, what would I write about? I didn't know much about anything beyond bouncing a basketball and prancing around in public in a pair of tight shorts. At my age, Hemingway had already been to war, sustained a serious wound and had a memorable love affair with an older woman. I had to learn something, *do* something, and acquire more life experience before I could hope to have anything worthwhile to write about.

Phil ended his days in Castro's Havana, having in 1975 published *Inside the Company: CIA Diary*, the infamous book that catapulted him into a perpetual flight for his safety. He'd had his say and forfeited any semblance of a normal life. He lost his wife and children and died a sick, lonely, drunken shell early in 2008.

But all of this came much later. After our school days we crossed paths during our military service in the late '50s and again in the late '60s when Phil was assigned to the CIA station in Mexico City and I was traveling with my friend and mentor, Bernie Tonnar, a Roman Catholic priest who was himself engaged in some unexplained academic/courier business of a covert nature. In fact, it was during this Mexican adventure that I acquired the base material for my first published novel.

Phil and I were to meet again in London in the early '70s, where he labored to complete his wretched name-revealing book and I struggled with my ongoing efforts to write saleable fiction. We both moved to Paris and then Spain at the same time but later struck out in separate directions. As a pair of disillusioned former government spooks, we had a good deal in common and no sure road ahead of us. We remained in contact through a number of mutual friends, and I expected him to be an important source of information for this book. But I couldn't travel to Cuba due to Darlene's deteriorating medical condition, and now that I have the time to move about, I find Phil to have been summoned to a previous engagement. May he rest in peace.

At least four other high school contemporaries that I am aware of became CIA officers and played important roles in events of the early sixties. To my knowledge, two are still alive. Contrary to Phil's inexcusable lapse of judgment in his book, I won't name these associates in this memoir.

PART FOUR

Call of the Jesuits

In September, 1948, George B. Mettler — the Barry was now silent — enrolled at Jesuit High School and set out to create his own persona.

From the beginning I loved Jesuit, the priests and scholastic staff and my fellow students, and they all seemed to accept me without reservation. The priests were wonderful teachers and role models, and a few became friends for life. Many years later a few priests of my acquaintance were enmeshed in the Church abuse controversies of that later time, but I'd never experienced any of it in my day.

The enrollment was fewer than three hundred boys that first year, and soon everyone knew each other by name. Phil Agee and Paul Antinori Jr. were classmates that first year and we developed good friendships.

What a time it was, 1948–49, to be embarking on my new adventure at Jesuit and having my mind and sensitivities opened to events outside the so-called Hell-Hole of the Gulf Coast. There really was a larger world out there, like all the places I had been reading about in my library books and encyclopedias. And with the guidance of the priests and other faculty members, I continued to pay close attention to world events and to make up private stories of my glorious participation in exciting deeds in far-off exotic lands.

In 1948, social, cultural and political turmoil extended all over Europe and beyond. Even far off in the Middle East, which all of us knew so little about in those days, there was suddenly a state of Israel. It was a nation where Jews could live, work and govern themselves as they saw fit. At least until other residents in the region advanced claims of their own to the sacred lands of Palestine.

And further away in China, Mao Tse-tung and his Communist revolutionaries had forced Chiang Kai-shek and his defeated forces into permanent exile to the island of Formosa. I wondered if any of mankind's nationalistic struggles would ever come to an end. I still wonder about such things.

Soon there was a dark cloud of fear massing overhead. I think it was the atomic bombs that Russia had recently tested. The world had hardly had a breather after the war, and here we were getting right back into belligerent confrontations with an aggressive world power.

The beach territories had long been a magnet for canny investors from all sections of the country, including the likes of Chicago's Al Capone and Johnny Torrio, Lucky Luciano and Meyer Lansky out of New York City, and Mickey Cohen from the West Coast regions. And of course, the tropical attributes of these virgin beach communities were not lost on such southern investors as the Carlos Marcello faction from across the Gulf in New Orleans, along with all of the heavy rollers

Meyer Lansky

in the Tampa Bay region. And Joseph P. Kennedy Sr. was investing heavily on Florida's east coast centering on the Palm Beach area. Real estate development had become as prominent a money-making venture for the syndicate barons as the importation and sale of drugs, alcohol and girls.

One afternoon I joined Phil Agee at a downtown soda fountain. I saw immediately that it was going to be another one of those discussions.

"Be straight with me, Georgie. Have they talked to you?"

"Who, the priests?"

He gave me a long, scrutinizing stare. "Well, they will, you might as well get ready. They're coming, and they're damned serious."

Before I could question him further, he was up from the table and gone. What the hell did that mean? Who were *they?* I would find out soon enough. The recruitment procession was about to begin.

The period from 1945 to 1950 had perhaps been the most pleasant interval in American history. But for me and for many Americans, the summer of 1950 would form a blistering memory, and not just because of excessive heat. Our national serenity was shattered on the night of June 25 when the North Korean Army swept down across the 38th Parallel into South Korea. Newspapers and radio told us the news; I didn't know anyone with a television set, didn't really know what TV was. Events moved rapidly. Within a week after the North Korean invasion, we were at war.

But how could this be? To most Americans, this wasn't like another Pearl Harbor. Nobody had attacked us. This was a civil war between two corrupt factions in an isolated island clear across the world. It had nothing to do with us; our national interest was not involved. We weren't in danger of attack, and there was no cause for all this alarm. We had movies to attend, the beach and our summer girls to occupy our attention. We just didn't understand what all the fuss was about.

Although there had been no declaration of war from the congress, President Truman said that it wasn't needed. He said this wasn't a war, that it was a "police action." There was a national draft in 1950, and our young men were once again placed in jeopardy.

One Friday afternoon later that semester, after history class, Mr. San Marco S. J., one of my favorite professors, made arrangements with me to meet him for brunch the next morning at a popular café on 7th Avenue in Ybor City. I felt awkward; a quick look around told me that I was the only Anglo in the place. Diners turned and looked at me as I made my way toward Mr. San Marco's table.

Social uncertainties were rampant in Tampa and Ybor City because of a recent unsolved murder of a leading figure in local syndicate operations. As soon as it became obvious to everyone that Mr. San Marco was my host, however, any hint of displeasure caused by my unexpected presence was extinguished.

"Good morning, Georgie. So glad you could come." He spoke with only the slightest accent and flashed his usual broad smile. Except for his Roman collar, he looked like the father or uncle of many of my friends in his sport coat, slacks and loafers. Talking resumed around us as I sat down.

"Wouldn't have missed it for the world," I said as a Cuban waiter graciously solicited our order. Mr. San Marco asked for a glass of draft beer from the local Tropical brewery and a glass of iced tea with lemon for me. For our lunch, we ordered hot Cuban sandwiches with sides of black beans and rice.

I had a visceral response to the atmosphere and pushed back in my chair to absorb the ambience of the café with its hardwood flooring, pristine white stucco walls, marble-topped tables and gleaming mahogany chairs. A large mirror behind the counter reflected a colorful mural across the room that depicted a scene out of rural Cuba. I'd always responded to the foreign, mysterious and slightly decadent ambience of our Latin Quarter. I liked my Latin friends and their special ways. I liked their food, drink and music. I liked the Old World architecture of the Quarter and the song-filled bistros. "I will bless our food," my host said. "We eat and then we talk." We did both, and then Mr. San Marco leaned across the table and drilled me with dark limpid eyes. "This collar allows me to be intrusive. Sure, you can clam up, ignore my effronteries, but you probably won't hit me."

I laughed, locked my hands together and told him to "Fire away."

He took a deep breath; this was going to be serious. "You are very young, Georgie, and your future is filled with promise. You are popular and deservedly so, and your best athletic days are ahead of you. You will accomplish much. But this is only the beginning; there is much yet to be done in order to secure your future. And there are so many snares along the path of development."

"Oh man, I ..."

"I am not speaking only about the girls. You are a smart boy. You will be faced with opportunities, approaches from unsuspected quarters. You have much to offer, but you must choose carefully and without haste."

What was he getting at? Did he know about that guy "Marteen" and his kind, the guys that had been hounding Phil Agee and me and a few of the other boys lately? Was this Mr. San Marco's way of warning me to steer clear of that world of light and shadow?

"Hopefully, you are young enough to avoid this Korean mess, but ..." He shrugged. "In any case, the military will not be your sole opportunity for service. There will be many ways in which you can serve your country, and, believe me, you will be solicited accordingly, and I just want you to prepare yourself. Do not be deceived by smooth talkers. Be smart; be wise. Make your mother proud."

He hesitated, marshaled his thoughts and leaned further across the table. "You have no money, Georgie, no family reputation to carry you forward. But you have one of the most precious treasures in life: you have good friends." His eyes were burning with the heat of sincerity. "Your heart is good, non-judgmental. But you must always remember who your real friends are. Never refuse help from a friend, and never refuse to give help to a friend in need."

He squeezed both of my wrists with enhanced emotion. "Now, Georgie, you are going to continue your education. You are going to Cuba."

He might as well have dashed the glass of beer into my face.

"No need to respond, it has all been arranged." He smiled broadly. "This is what friends are for."

Looking back now, I see that this was the time when the earth really began to shift beneath my feet. A few days after the Cuba bombshell had rattled my composure, our mystery man, the one called Martin, presented himself in clear focus in his room at the Floridian Hotel, a prestigious hotel in downtown Tampa.

By now I'd seen him twice before when his face was covered by dark sunglasses and a drooping panama hat. This time I got a clear look at him and wasn't impressed. His blond hair was thinning, his complexion sun-ravaged and his eyes glazed by an excess of booze. I searched in vain for any redeeming features.

He swallowed half a glass of gin and reached for the bottle. "You come very highly recommended," he said, and I wondered where I'd heard *that* before. But this guy was no Roman Catholic priest come to call.

"I wish we could have dined in more comfort downstairs, but public restaurants have eyes and ears," he said as we settled down over steaks and potatoes that had been served by a discreet waiter who I assumed was not part of the hotel wait staff.

I didn't know how much liquor Martin had consumed prior to my arrival, but he would soon be lit. I was nervous as a cat and just waited him out. Martin smiled. "You're a careful lad, I like that. Always know who you are talking with before giving anything away."

"I don't know anything about you. And I don't know what I have to give away."

"Oh, you know enough. That's why I'm talking to you."

He shoved a giant piece of steak into his mouth and said, "Word has it that you have a good ear for Spanish and an affinity for the Latin culture. That's good; we need people with such capabilities."

I swallowed hard and asked, "Just who is *we?*"

He glared at me over his gin fix. Was this a mistake? Was he just going to throw me out and keep both steaks to himself? Or was he going to have my knees — what did they call it on the street — capped?

"We work for the president of the United States," he said after a thoughtful pause and stirred the ice in his drink with his forefinger. The man was an unmistakable slob. "Harry has stuck us in the Asian mud, but Ike will soon take charge." Dwight Eisenhower was expected to head the Republican ticket in the next election. "Ike knows more about our business than any man in or out of government. Don't ever let the grandfatherly persona fool you."

I wasn't fooled by this smarmy persona either.

"You still haven't told me what business you — any of you — are in: pharmaceuticals, hardware, or women's lingerie?" I suppose I was feeling my oats since he hadn't pistol-whipped me yet.

He laughed at this, really laughed. "You're good, kid, really good. Were you a little older, I'd give you a drink or three." He cleared his throat and his eyes went flint-hard. "But now let's get down to business."

And he laid it on the table. I had valuable assets, he repeated. I was smart, athletic and catnip to the girls, and all of that could be very useful. I looked and I saw things, he said, and that too was good. He said there was no rush, there was plenty of time.

Another year of high school, then college and maybe some graduate work. And maybe some intensive language study."

"And maybe the U.S. Army," I suggested.

He shrugged. "Military obligations can be managed. Service is service, in more ways than one. Uniforms aren't the only way to serve your country."

I wondered if Agee had received this same sales pitch. But somehow the conversation veered over to my most recent scoring title and whether or not I thought old Hemingway would ever win the Nobel Prize for Literature. He poured himself more gin, and I figured that whatever he was up to, he'd been satisfied with the night's work.

At the door we shook hands, and he massaged my shoulder with his free hand in a gesture that made my flesh crawl. I couldn't help thinking of the soldier who had moved on me that night near the war's end, and I hoped that Santo Jr. was lurking protectively somewhere out in the corridor.

Soon thereafter — I'd scarcely had time to digest the contents of my meeting with Martin — I was on my way to what was then called the "Paris of the Antilles," a pleasure paradise situated a scant ninety miles off the coast of Florida. It had all been arranged. Exactly by whom, I never fully understood. But there was good cover for my trip. I would ride down to Miami with two of my best friends and fellow teammates, Jimmy La Russa and Cookie Garcia, in Jimmy's car.

Jimmy had been recruited by the University of Miami football program and would sign a four-year scholarship. Cookie hailed from a Cuban family of considerable prominence in both countries. His older brother would become a respected judge in Dade County, Florida, and one of his cousins, who was born and raised in Cuba, would become known to the world as Andy Garcia, one of the prominent Hollywood stars of *The Godfather* movie saga. Cookie's family was and remains in the shipping business, moving produce in and out of Cuba and the Caribbean basin to and from the United States.

We knifed down through the Everglades into Miami, settled into our hotel for lunch, and then moved off on our separate missions. I excitedly headed off for my prearranged dockside rendezvous. I expected to then receive my itinerary instructions as to the imminent crossing to Havana.

"Aqui!" A man waved from a canopied table at a popular outdoor café. He wore the customary white *guayabera* shirt loose at the waist, dark trousers, black and white two-tone shoes, and a white panama hat. He was already drinking beer, the ever-popular *Cervesa* Tropical, and I ordered a Coke. I wondered if anyone else was joining us.

"Buenas tardes," he said. "Good afternoon."

"Y usted," I replied; my antenna was up and pulsing.

My host introduced himself as Artice Valez. "There have been changes to the plan," he said in a low, rather conspiratorial voice made sinister by the heavy Cuban pronunciation.

The patio was crowded with diners, and I sat there with my stomach in turmoil as he explained that political affairs in Cuba were in a state of flux and that a new election was coming soon. Mr. San Marco had summarized all of this for me before I left Tampa, and I'd spent a couple of hours in research in the public library. The next election would take place in 1952, and former president Fulgencio Batista and his military henchmen were expected to win.

I was aware of the gaseous political turmoil that was building steam across the island. That was one reason that I wanted to go there, before it was perhaps too late. Admittedly, things were bad enough already.

Velez finally ran down; the history lesson was over. "As you can see, this is not the time for such a visit as was planned. Affairs are too uncertain." He finished his beer, stood, resettled his hat and looked at me apologetically. "I am only the messenger, *comprende?"*

I nodded and watched as he walked off in the direction of the boats berthed in the marina and couldn't help wondering which one would have been mine. The first truly great adventure of my life had died stillborn.

Later that night I tried to ameliorate my regret in the midst of a boisterous crowd at a lively downtown tavern on Flagler Street. I didn't know where Jimmy and Cookie were, but Phil Agee was at the table. The talk was loud and often passionate.

"It will come, I'm telling you," Phil said, "with or without this young firebrand." A young law student at the University of Havana named Fidel Castro had been making incendiary, well-attended speeches off and on during the summer, using improvised podiums all along Flagler Street.

"The way things are in Cuba today, revolution can't be avoided," Phil said. "With Batista on his way back into power, the Fat Cats from the U.S. and abroad will regain their old sandbox for plunder. But it's my sense that the Cuban people won't put up with it this time around."

I could see what Phil was getting at and I think I agreed with him. Artice Velez would certainly have agreed. Beneath the shiny veneer, a pervasive corruption simmered that was destined to lead to unimagined change and turmoil.

More beer came, and a girl leaned over me from behind and put her tongue in my ear. "Wanta go for a walk?" she whispered, but before I could even turn around a wag across the table said, "Not to worry, *amigos*. Ol' Hemin'way won't allow anything to ruin his cozy little island habitat. I hear he's already writing a new story: "The Short Unhappy Life of Fidel Castro."

The greatest American writer of that day — perhaps of any day — maintained an island getaway that he called the *Finca Vigia* (Lookout Farm) in San Francisco de Paula, near Havana.

Phil got up, touched my shoulder in passing and nodded out toward the sidewalk. I caught up with him, and he turned to me without any preliminaries.

"I was going over, too. But it really is for the best that we don't go right now. We'll cross later. We'll go when the time is right. Now tell me, who set it up for you, him, our guy Martin? Or are they coming at us in relays now?"

"I don't want to talk about this stuff anymore, Phil. I'm through with all of it."

Either he believed I was truly cold to what he was talking about, or I was maintaining cover even in the face of our friendship. He smiled and walked away.

****

Fred Osborn and I had a breakfast meeting at a roadside café near the Missouri line. "You were in Florida in 1961, in law school during the days before and after the Bay of Pigs fiasco — right?"

"Right," I replied and was immediately on the alert for what might follow.

"And in the Army, you were C.O. of a security unit at the U.S. atomic weapons training post out there on the west Texas–Mexican border in the late fifties. It was a top-secret operation that hosted military, intelligence, and scientific specialists from allied countries around the world — right?"

I shifted nervously in my seat and said, somewhat testily, "Ft. Bliss, yeah. You know all of this, Fred, it's in my record. What are you …?"

"*Some* of it is in your record. You met all sorts of high-ranking individuals from our country and abroad. I know you were solicited to provide men from your unit for certain special tests then being conducted under deepest cover over in Mexico."

This was totally unexpected. I'd never had this discussion about those days in the desert with anyone. I knew he had to be referring to the government's MK–ULTRA program, a drug-induced mind control program of patent inhumanity and illegality, but I wasn't going to go down into that snake pit again, not willingly. I'd been down there, and I didn't intend ever to go back.

"Okay, settle down. I know you turned them all down — especially the approaches of that long-time friend of yours — what do you call him — Marvin?"

Jesus Christ! I thought, is this why Fred has befriended me all this time? I remembered the photos that he'd sprung on me that night — photos of Santo Jr. and Carlos Marcello. Did he have a photo of Martin to nail me with? Was Fred running some sort of covert operation that had somehow come to be focused on me? The thought made my flesh crawl.

But Fred only laughed at my spontaneous reaction. "Guy's a piece of work, and if you haven't already run aground, you'll do well to keep a wide birth." He paused and drew a deep breath, and suddenly I realized that none of this was coming easy to him either. "At any time in your career so far — Army or Bureau — have you ever heard of the 5412 Committee?"

Now he may as well have poured his cup of scalding coffee into my lap. Yes, I'd damned well heard of the Committee. I'd had a number of discreet conversations with a team of CIA agents engaged in some sort of undisclosed operation out there in the Texas–New Mexico desert, all of whom made no secret of the fact that they would be happy to recruit me into service with the Company. I liked them; they were of an entirely different caliber than the Martin creep who had been hounding me for so long. The National Security Council's 5412 Committee, they had informed me under terms of deepest confidentiality, was the small group that had been empowered by the National Security Act of 1947 to direct covert operations for the United States, which they did by way of their designated Special Group.

The Committee consisted of the president, the secretaries of State and Defense, the chairman of the Joint Chiefs of Staff and the director of the CIA. It was and is the most powerful and secret committee of the U.S. government. Its capacity to wage covert, secret war was limited to the discretion of these few individuals, only one of whom, the president, was elected by the American people. It was labeled "ultrasensitive," the only classification above the "top secret" level that I carried. Very few citizens have ever heard of it, even today, and that morning I damned sure wished that I wasn't among that select group. Where the hell was Fred going with this?

"Come on, Fred — what's this all about?"

He studied me intently for some moments and then said, "I just don't know what you know, or how much you might know that *I* don't know." My stomach was roiling with jet streams of paranoid acid. Where would he take this? Out to El Paso, Juarez, Mexico City? How much did Fred know about my Army days and what would he do with the information that he possessed?

"You do know that JFK took the blame for the failure at the Bay of Pigs. His refusal to authorize air cover, they said, *that's* what caused the debacle. It's all public knowledge today. And apparently it's all public bullshit!"

I'd never seen Fred so exercised; he was really pissed.

"The way I understand it, it was all a setup, and Kennedy walked right into it. The 5412 had placed authority for covert operations in the hands of the Select Committee. They knew how crucial the last-minute air coverage was. But they also knew that by the terms of 5412, peacetime operations against a foreign nation could not be conducted by U.S. *military* forces. Rather, the CIA was empowered to conduct all such clandestine operations with discreet military support actions that would afford plausible deniability should the operation become public knowledge."

"So JFK could not have constitutionally ordered U.S. military air support at the Bay of Pigs. Is that what you're saying?"

"That's what I'm saying. Jack had ordered covert *non-military* support that final day, but after he had gone to bed, the bombing mission was cancelled at the last minute by a member of the Special Group or his own staff; I don't know who specifically. And remember, none of this was Jack's plan at all, not ever." He saw the shock on my face and said, "It had been dumped on his desk ready to go when he took office. Ike, Nixon and Dulles — it was their project, monitored all the way by the outgoing 5412 Committee and its Special Group."

Allen Dulles, former director of the CIA, was sacked by JFK for incompetence after the invasion debacle. I just couldn't respond. I was sunk into a pit of shocked silence.

"Remember, they'd all wanted, expected, Nixon to win the election. So now the Cuba failure would serve as some insurance that JFK would not be reelected in '64. That was their thinking. And today those same goddamned bozos over at the Company are apparently yoked in a continuing alliance with your old wiseguy *compadres* to assassinate Castro and overthrow the regime in Cuba. But, and this is the $64 question, is this operation just another setup designed to blow up in President Kennedy's face?"

We didn't know how close to the truth Fred was. But in the end we would find that the scheme was even more convoluted than either of us could have imagined.

****

Home is the sailor, home from the sea. But this sailor never even made it aboard ship.

My disappointment in not getting to Cuba back in that summer of 1950, however, was soon mitigated by events. Remember, there was a war going on in a distant land that was killing and maiming our boys.

And it had become obvious by now to everyone with an ounce of common sense that the United States was not prepared for a war anywhere. We had no combat weapons, no tanks, and absolutely no capability of combating a serious and well-prepared combat force, which the North Koreans had proved to be. We had nothing but bluster and racist arrogance.

But were matters unfolding exactly according to plans of the 5412 Committee, which at that time I, or anyone that I knew, had never heard of? What could have been their motivation? In all likelihood, money and power; I was already beginning to learn that these two indispensable ingredients went together. Money begets power, and power begets money in a bigamous cycle. But what had begun as a supposed walk in the park was turning into a military nightmare for our ill-prepared troops. It was one of the worst periods in U.S. military history, and all of Washington, President Truman included, was said to be in traumatic shock.

Most Americans, however, still had not come to take the war seriously. Only those parties who were poised to reap millions of dollars in armament sales while expecting billions before it was all over were content with present conditions. Most Americans couldn't understand the Korean place names and had no clear idea where Korea actually was. Guys at school had a simple enough solution: "Let the goddamn Gooks kill each other. Nobody else can tell 'em apart anyway."

Fighting had raged on into late summer and fall, and a number of older boys that I knew in the community had been called up; but so far there had been no local deaths. Then suddenly we were immersed not only in the fight in Korea, but also in a splenetic verbal war against Communism right here at home and around the world.

The crusade had begun back in the late '40s, and now radio and newspapers sounded a daily alarm. Almost overnight the Red

Scare was officially upon us. It wasn't just Korea, the Communists were everywhere. We had to watch out for Reds, pinkos, fellow travelers, the damnable New Dealers and all the slimy liberals so intent upon overturning the U.S. Constitution.

At Jesuit, of course, the Fathers were officially against the evil of Communism. There was even a recent papal encyclical called Atheistic Communism that summoned the faithful into lockstep. This meant support for the deceitful rantings of U.S. Senators Joseph McCarthy and Richard Nixon, and the vitriolic congressman, J. Parnell Thomas, Chairman of the House Un-American Activities Committee (HUAC).

And what a joy it was for me in later life to co-represent Thomas in high-level corporate litigation with substantial damages at stake, a suit based upon his perjury and financial duplicity; a suit which, I am pleased to say, we lost. Thomas was as ruined thereafter in business and reputation as the thousands of innocent targets of his scandalous committee hearings throughout the early fifties.

But the Red Scare wasn't the only media show in Tampa for our local and international entertainment. In 1951, Senator Estes Kefauver had come to town with his traveling road circus called the Senate Special Committee for Investigating Crime in Interstate Commerce, popularly known as the Kefauver Committee. Its mission was supposed to have been to plumb the depths of organized crime in America. In reality, it was little more than a public relations gimmick with cameras and press reporters in attendance, all designed to boost Kefauver's presidential aspirations.

But, thanks to television, it had also served to make the word "Mafia" a household name in America. Although I was personally not to see a television program for another three years, the nation was mesmerized by this new technical innovation that featured the dramatic appearance on screen of reputed mobsters such as Frank Costello and his sweaty hands, Albert Anastasia and Mickey Cohen. There had already been hearings in Chicago, St. Louis, San Francisco, New Orleans and a dozen or so other cities, all showcasing the crusading Tennessean with his ridiculous coonskin cap.

The hearings in Tampa had put our city on the national map. "Hell-Hole of the Gulf Coast," the media referred to us again, along with "City of Blood" and "Little Chicago." FBI Director Hoover could proclaim that there was no Mafia until he turned blue in the face, but there was a Mafia, and now the country and the world knew it, had seen it with their own eyes. Television had made the seemingly unknowable real to one and all.

Even Santo Sr. and Santo Jr. were issued Senate subpoenas, but both had dodged the call, leaving town and invoking their Fifth Amendment right to remain silent. But their names, like that of the Mafia itself, were now a nationally known commodity. Henceforth father and son would become more reclusive than ever.

One night, not long after the hearings had concluded, I was riding my bicycle around the corner to the drugstore. Some of my neighborhood buddies were there, but feeling the need to be alone, I rode on. I turned onto Columbus Drive and rode on down toward the river. I found myself at the corner of Columbus and North Boulevard and decided to ride on over to Jax Cookies and get Mama a bag of the fresh-baked oatmeal cookies that she so enjoyed. After a couple of blocks, I met Santo Jr.

Jesus, I thought. What's he doing out here at night walking by himself?

"Hey, kid!" He waved to me from across the street.

I was to learn later that, unlike most other Mafia leaders, Santo had no official bodyguards. Not in Tampa, not in this day. Here he was often seen driving and walking alone, unhurried and apparently unworried about his physical safety.

"Mind the traffic," he warned as I crossed the road, seemingly as skittish as Mama used to be, but traffic was light and I reached the far curb without mishap. It was a hot, steamy night, but he was dressed as if he was about to make a speech to the local Chamber of Commerce. And behind the horn rimmed glasses his friendly eyes shone out of the shadows like green searchlights.

"Where's your wagon, kid?" He saw my confusion and laughed. "Not a kid anymore, hey Barry? Oh, I mean, Georgie."

He had such a way of putting you at ease, this criminal eminence of growing legend, that I laughed too, remembering the night toward the end of the war when he came to my aide. I'd seen and talked with him many times since that night but one-on-one conversations had been rare. He'd always spoken pleasantly to me though, and he did seem like a friend.

"Good season on the court. Fine outside shot, and you run the lanes real good." He spoke in a soft voice with almost no accent. "Share the ball good, too. Teamwork is all important."

"Thanks, Mr. Trafficante."

I didn't know what else to say. Me, talking with the Mafia don of all creation! When his father died, he would be the Man.

"We friends, Georgie — you call me Santo."

I nodded, swallowed hard and said, "Santo," almost in a whisper.

"Too bad about your trip south. Things don't always work out the first time, but you'll get there."

So, he knew about my aborted trip to Cuba. But I wasn't really surprised. I should have known that it wasn't just Mr. San Marco pulling the strings, or Martin. Santo's hand must have been involved. Had he even been behind my recruitment to Jesuit? Would I ever know the answers to such questions? I nodded and fidgeted about on my bike, unsure what to say to him about Cuba.

"Better go on home now, it's getting late. Don't want to worry your dear mother. Late for me, too — enough exercise for one night."

And he walked off, smiling, toward his house a few blocks away. Killer? Drug merchant? Political fixer? Or admired hometown friend?

Only when I got home did I realize I'd forgotten to stop for Mama's cookies.

Of course, there were responsive Americans hopeful of influencing our government in more constructive ways than had been evidenced by current trends. One young northeastern congressman stressed the importance of foreign affairs in the welfare of our national future. It was his specific hope, he said, that the United States might develop nonmilitary forms of resistance against totalitarian forces of opposition rather than reacting in knee-jerk responses, such as our present-day self-destructive reflex performance in Korea.

But would anyone listen to such a sensible voice of reason? The congressman's name was John F. Kennedy, the young naval officer of PT-109 fame.

Still, in spite of the worry about Korea, Communists in our midst, and gangsters running rampant through our streets, it was a wonderful place to be young in 1951. Sure, there were troubles at home and in the world, but we had other concerns. We had our lives to get on with. I'd had a good social life all year. Athletic success and notoriety helped. I dated a few girls from the neighborhood and more than a few from Sacred Heart Academy and the Holy Name Academy. Nothing hot and serious, mind you. Remember the times; these were good Catholic girls. We might dance and pet lightly on Friday and Saturday nights, but Sunday morning would find them in church kneeling in the confessional booth.

But in the spring of that year at our Junior-Senior prom, I fell in love for the first time in my life. Not with my date, but with a girl dancing across the room with one of my good friends. She was almost indescribably beautiful with curly brown hair shot through with golden tints, and her figure was that of a fairy princess. The music was wonderful, and her eyes met mine over the shoulders and heads of our respective dates.

Her name was Sally Villar, and I'd actually known her in grammar school. But we weren't close in those early days, and I hadn't seen her again until the night of the prom dance. I phoned her the next day, and we both just assumed that we would be together forever. Nat King Cole's "They Tried to Tell Us We're Too Young" was our theme song, along with Tony Bennett's "Because of You."

But as good as life was because of new-found love, there was still Korea.

****

The ugly, pointless ground struggle slogged on in "the sour little war" that was ultimately to claim more than 50,000 American casualties. It was making a mockery of our so-called military superiority and would drag on for two more years. But my high school experience was winding down. What was my future? Mama and Sally, of course, hoped to keep me close to home. Maybe attend the University of Tampa, major in business and later enter the auto parts business with Sally's successful father. Knowing what you have already learned about me, you can imagine that such an itinerary didn't exactly thrill me.

I'd received a number of scholarship queries and offers from athletic programs around the country and then, one night shortly before graduation, I was paid a visit by the head coach at Loyola University of the South, located in New Orleans. I eagerly met one evening with Coach Tom Haggerty in his room at the elegant Tampa Terrace Hotel in downtown Tampa.

It was an awesome prospect to be courted by the coach who had won a national championship while coaching at Loyola of Chicago just a few years earlier. With limited preliminaries, he offered me a four-year scholarship that would never cost my family so much as a dime. Although I was stunned, I was not rendered quite speechless: I said yes.

PART FIVE

New Orleans: Land of Dreams

Although I don't know the exact point at which I began to assimilate the feel of wonder about the new life that awaited me, by the time we entered the historic old city of story and legend I was transfixed by the sights, sounds and smells of this land of dreams. Here was a real city of dreams and illusions; a city to escape from and to escape to.

New Orleans!

Whatever you are looking for can be found in New Orleans. You might even receive more than you really want and far more than what is good for you. Or it may be the commencement of a new life.

I was sitting straight up on the back seat, ready to learn, as John turned onto Calhoun Street, which bounded one side of the campus of Loyola University. He stopped in front of number 1722, a large unpainted, weather-worn house with a wooden staircase rising from the sidewalk to a wide covered porch, and I was struck by the realization that *this* was my new home.

The house was appropriately called the Ranch House. It was an animal farm. It was an unofficial insane asylum housing the most eccentric, fantastic, outrageous and wonderful bunch of lunatics it has ever been my privilege to know.

The older boys, mostly a mob of hoodlums from Chicago, clustered together near the front of the house. Ed Galvin and Ed "Skeets" Tuohy shared a room. Skeets' uncle was "Roger the Terrible" Tuohy, the only Chicago gangster who Al Capone ever publicly said he feared. (Skeets' son, Sean, is the husband of Leigh Anne Tuohy, the inspiration for the recent Academy Award-winning film, *The Blind Side*.) Galvin became my best friend and mentor, the older brother I never had and had wished for all of my life. He was the best influence on my life for the three years that we were together and remains my oldest living friend to this day.

So here we were, fourteen eccentric misfits gathered together in one house. The student body was always on the alert for what might happen next over at the fun house on Calhoun Street. And although the Ranch House was notorious well before my arrival, I did nothing to improve its reputation during the four years of my commitment.

I wish I could recall the words and events exactly as they transpired, but 1952 was a long time ago in another world. This is, therefore, a pastiche of my experiences, dreams, ambitions and disappointments during an eventful period like no other in our nation's history. Hindsight allows us to see that no other time has registered such profound changes, social, political and cultural, that as yet remain unassimilated by the general body politic in matters large and small, as those that occurred during the decades of the '50s and '60s. But how could I have known what the future held in store for me? How could I possibly have imagined the roles that many of my new and older acquaintances would play in my life and in the future of our country?

Although many of the names meant little or nothing to me at the time, how many fuzzy-headed college students could claim acquaintanceship with such figures as Mafia godfathers Santo Trafficante and Carlos Marcello; the likes of *agents provocateurs* David Ferrie, Guy Banister, Jack Ruby and Clay Shaw; and the pitiful Lee Harvey Oswald; along with district attorney Jim Garrison and his chief assistant Frank Klein, a good college friend of mine. All of these characters were to play significant roles in the social turmoil of the days, months and years to come; turmoil that included criminal corruption, war, and multiple assassinations.

But this was New Orleans, this was my new world, and I was happy in it. And if New Orleans wasn't the center of the universe, it was the magnetic pole of America during the 1950s. Like Paris between the two world wars, New Orleans in that day was a golden bowl.

Even prior to leaving Tampa, I had spent hours in the public library researching the history of the city and reviewing underworld intrigue as far west as Dallas, Texas.

The New Orleans clan was the oldest Mafia family in America, having been established in the mid-1800s. Largely because Louisiana's climate was similar to that in Sicily, immigrants from the old country preferred New Orleans to all other American port cities, including New York City.

By the late forties, Carlos Marcello had become the undisputed head of the family. Marcello ruled with an iron hand, or fist, and had become the boss of a two-billion-dollar annual empire. Barely five feet tall and semi-literate, the little man maintained control over New Orleans using bribery, subversion, intimidation, violence, murder and mayhem.

The New Orleans Mafia operated as a law unto itself. Prior to his arrival in Tampa, Senator Estes Kefauver, brought his dog-and-pony show to the Crescent City and focused on Carlos Marcello, whom the senator had labeled "the evil genius of organized crime in Louisiana." And although Marcello appeared before the committee, he exercised his sacrosanct Constitutional right not to answer incriminating questions. He invoked his Fifth Amendment privilege more than a hundred times during the hearings, including when asked his legal name, date and place of birth, current occupation, religious affiliation and marital status. In utter frustration, the embattled senator had demanded that Marcello state for the record what laws he had violated against the state of Louisiana and the United States of America.

"Ya betta had ast my attorneys dat kinda question," Marcello answered in his unique Louisiana accent. "Dat be what I pay 'em for."

Kefauver had been outraged by the man's boorish conduct and had him cited for Contempt of Congress. Marcello had been convicted and sentenced to serve six months in jail. The conviction and sentence, however, had been overturned on appeal on the grounds that any witness was entirely within his constitutional rights to refuse to testify.

Most fun-loving Louisianans agreed that no man should be publicly forced to admit whether or not he was married!

It wouldn't be long before I would make acquaintances with many such people in this rarefied milieu, often by way of my previous Tampa connections.

The French Quarter was our university: the nights, the days, the adventures. Not even Ybor City in Tampa had prepared me for the visceral reaction that I experienced to New Orleans. I immersed myself in the culture, and traditions. I loved the streets and byways, the music, the exotic language — the lilt, rhythms and dialects of Creole, Cajun, the port cities, and wide plains of Africa.

****

New Orleanians to this day live by one rule: "*Laissez les bon temps rouler.*" (Let the good times roll.) It was soon clear to me that to a bona fide New Orleanian, evil is a fact of life, as is goodness. In the "City That Care Forgot" sin hangs overhead like riffs of jazz carried on the mist floating in from the bayous on a muggy summer night. Crime and corruption are as ordinary as faith and charity.

The Marcello enterprise operated out of headquarters in the family-owned Town and Country Motel and Restaurant situated on the garish Airline Highway. The scandalous revelations that had resulted from the earlier Kefauver hearings had caused Marcello to shut down his original operation across the river at Willswood Tavern. The abandoned headquarters was currently nothing more than a restaurant owned by Marcello's mother and managed by Al Capone's former chef.

The trendy nightspot on the Airline Highway — a favorite of the college crowd — was now the meeting place for members of Marcello's corrupt organization and the crooked politicians and law enforcement officials who served and protected him. The New Orleans Police Department was said to be so corrupt that nearly every member of the force collected and distributed graft.

The Chief of Police was the uncle of one of my college teammates. And one of the department heads was an alcoholic right-wing fanatic and former FBI agent named Guy Banister, who would soon be dismissed from the force for a public act of drunken violence.

And the roster of corrupt officials included the Mayor of New Orleans, who was said to owe his election to the mob and served as a bag-man for the clan's bookmaking operations in the French Quarter, operations supervised in part by one Dutz Murret, the father of another teammate and the uncle of Lee Harvey Oswald, which means that Oswald was the nephew of a Mafia functionary.

Meanwhile the litany goes on and on. Allegedly, the mob dominated the state police, the entire state bureaucracy, the governor's office, many of the judiciary and district attorneys, a powerful U.S. senator, and at least one influential congressman. All under the control of one semi-literate Sicilian

The motel/restaurant complex showcased an exotic *ramboule* of slot machines, gaming rooms, a first-class restaurant and bar, B-girls and prostitutes. There was a spacious dance floor and the non-stop music of a quality band. It was managed by Marcello associates and by his youngest brother, Anthony, a friend and confidant to much of the college crowd.

A horseracing wire network that was tied into the Mafia-owned national network was operated from the back rooms, providing racing tips and results to bookies throughout the country. Fixed races took place here and around the country every day. Marcello's personal secretary, Miss Frances, supervised a call-girl ring extending across the entire Southeast and focusing on the nearby Naval Air Station in Biloxi, Mississippi. Every payday she bused the girls down to their positions outside the station gates in time for the stampede. Miss Frances rented rooms appropriate to the occasion all over the area, and none ever passed an unused hour. Back in the Town and Country the next night, grateful toasts were always offered up to the U.S. Navy. Some of us at the Ranch House called this operation the "Quail Run."

It wasn't long before the Ranch House gang was socializing comfortably in this colorful environment, and once the management realized that the friendship of Santo Trafficante had preceded my arrival in the city, I operated with a cache that none of the older guys enjoyed.

In the coming weeks, I witnessed such mob luminaries — known to most citizens now, thanks to all the Kefauver publicity — as Frank Costello (his son regularly dated one of my best college friends), Meyer Lansky, Joseph Cimino (Marcello's man in Dallas), "Diamond Jim" Moran, aka James Brocatto, Frank Coppola, Paul Kastle and none other than "Uncle Earle" himself, Earl Long, the soon to become whacko governor of Louisiana and his talented companion, stripper Blaze Starr.

Occasionally Santo Trafficante Jr. and his Tampa entourage would show up. The warm personal treatment that I received from Santo and the others rendered me socially acceptable in such circles for the rest of my college days. This is not meant to suggest that I was ever an intimate friend of Santo Trafficante. I'm not even certain that he had any intimate friends, not in the common sense of the expression. I suspect that all of his relationships, even those with his peers, were more a matter of business than friendship.

But this is hindsight. Back in those college days, I was still incapable of such an assessment of Santo's character. Certainly it never crossed my mind that he had any ulterior motive for being generous toward me, that he might feel that in the future this kid from the old neighborhood might be of some service to him.

Another of my compatriots from Tampa, Paul Antinori Jr., was a fellow freshman at Loyola. But unlike during our days together at Jesuit, we had little contact with each other now. His pursuits took him one way and mine took me another. I have already told you that Paul became a successful lawyer, prosecutor, and sometime attorney for Santo Trafficante Jr. I became ...

****

I couldn't go home that first Christmas; there was basketball practice and the season was upon us. I hadn't yet realized that all the practice in the world would have little bearing on my position on the roster. If Coach Haggerty had a major failing, it was his compulsion to offer far too many scholarships to talented prospects around the country. After all, a basketball team consists of only five players who can be on the court at one time. There was no way he could fit us all into significant playing time.

I was okay with the situation. I was having such meaningful experiences with my books (not school books), movies, girls, and the magic city that I didn't give anything else much thought.

About this time a newspaper article caught my interest concerning that former PT boat hero from the war — John Kennedy — who after the war had been elected to the House of Representatives and then to the U.S. Senate and was now being referred to in the media as the "Senate's Gay Young Bachelor."

I didn't pay it much attention, having a much greater interest in the senate "Red-Hater" commonly referred to as "Tail-gunner Joe" McCarthy. A move in the Senate to censure him was picking up steam and as a journalism aspirant, this was of continuing interest to me.

Lt. John F. Kennedy (right) with Crew on PT 109

Now, having maintained only slight communication with anyone in Tampa during the first semester, I was shocked to learn from fellow-Tampan Don Rodriguez that shortly after the first of the year Santo Jr. had been the target of a hit attempt back home. Rod didn't have any details, however, except that Santo was not seriously injured, and the shooters got away.

Meanwhile my experiences in New Orleans were heating up to the boiling point. Are you familiar with the great French writer Colette's advice? We would all do foolish things, she wrote, but we should do them with enthusiasm. Well, most of the Ranch House hoodlums had never heard of Colette but were ripe with enthusiasm. We would routinely hop a streetcar on St. Charles Avenue in front of the University and ride to Canal Street, and then cross over into the Quarter on Bourbon Street to enter the demiworld of Tennessee Williams, Faulkner and Capote. Many of the bars, restaurants and strip clubs were owned or controlled by the Marcello mob family, and our access was free and easy in spite of our relatively tender ages.

One night I split off from the other guys and found myself in the cocktail lounge of one of the Quarter's most prestigious hotels where I met a lovely young French movie actress, whom I shall refer to as Monique Monet. She had recently enjoyed a bit role in a popular Hollywood movie about WWII, but her career had subsequently stalled, and to make ends meet she was playing the circuit of cocktail lounges around the country. Tonight, after her final performance, I found her seated at the bar alone and depressed, on the verge of having three or four too many. We talked and became friends for the remaining three nights of her New Orleans commitment.

Now jumping ahead a year or two, he appeared at the Tropicana Hotel in Havana and was asked to join the table of a pair of distinguished patrons, clearly friends of the owner of the hotel, Santo Trafficante Jr. Both young men were members of the U.S. Senate and were captivated by Monique's charm and beauty.

One man, George Smathers, was decidedly Southern in speech and manner, while the other, John Kennedy, was handsome and fair-haired and exhibited the distinct speech patterns of Boston's Back Bay. After a few complimentary drinks, Monique spent the rest of the night in the intimate company of a future president of the United States. I always wished for an opportunity to compliment Mr. K. on his taste and to razz him that I had been there first, but I never quite got the chance.

The war in Korea raged on, filling most Americans with the growing apprehension that it was the prelude to World War III. Communism had become the overriding national political issue. President Truman insisted that there was not a single Communist or otherwise disloyal person in the United States government, and Senator Joe McCarthy brayed the outrageous lie that he was in possession of a list of names numbering in the hundreds regarding traitors in the U.S. State Department. Nor was the House of Representatives to be outdone by the Senate. The Un-American Activities Committee, under the leadership of its vitriolic chairman J. Parnell Thomas, my future client, regularly trampled the U.S. Constitution in the name of justice, patriotism and national security.

And even while Cardinal Spellman spewed his right-wing venom from his ermine-draped pulpit, yet another matter in which most of the country could take little pleasure was foisted upon the republic as a result of these tumultuous years. Richard M. Nixon came roaring out of the West onto the national scene in the guise of America's number-one defender of the faith. Now the modern witch hunt was under way with Nixon, McCarthy, Thomas and Spellman leading the charge. Jobs and careers were destroyed, reputations tarnished, lives ruined and lost. Ordinary men and women lived in daily fear of anonymous accusation followed by government scrutiny, both overt and covert.

It was one of the most shameful interludes in American history, and looking back you can see that it was an unpropitious time to pursue one's education. And yet here we were, a pack of student athletes with the world by the tail. Very few of my friends to my recollection ever worried about such matters, much less pursued them in any sort of heated discourse. There was no Phil Agee among the denizens of the Ranch House, or, if there were, he was operating under the deepest cover.

****

Summer came and most of us headed off for visitations in our respective hometowns. Phil Agee was also home for summer vacation from Notre Dame. We huddled together for a good talk. "Yeah, yeah," he said over hamburgers and Cokes, "it's cold in South Bend, and there are no girls on campus."

I laughed. "It's not so cold in New Orleans, but the girls are for the most part off-limits. On their knees for prayer service morning, noon and night."

"On their knees for service all right." He tossed a soggy French fry at me and said, "Okay, has *he* talked with you? Have any of them talked with you?"

I stiffened. "You ask that every time we get together."

"And you evade answering every time I ask." I laughed but Phil wasn't laughing. "What about that guy in New Orleans, that Banister fellow? You know him?"

"I run into him around the Quarter now and again. I don't *know* him."

"Better make it your business to get to know him," he said emphatically and had now gained my undivided attention. "Besides being a virulent racist, he's a commie hater of Orwellian proportions. And he really likes to recruit college students for his …"

"Phil, I have *not* been recruited by Banister, *Marteen,* or anybody else. And I don't want to be recruited."

He continued like he hadn't even heard me. "He's ex-FBI, OSS and Naval Intelligence, see. And he's no good."

"Thanks for telling me."

"*Warning* you. He *will* come calling, they *all* will. You're fair game."

We paid our bill and walked outside into the golden sunshine.

"You know OSS is now defunct and has been replaced by CIA."

"Have *you* signed up?"

"Close," he said, and as he turned the corner away from me he called out over his shoulder, "Keep alert, Georgie, they *are* cruising."

I walked around in circles for a few moments. What the hell did any of this have to do with me? I wasn't *looking* to be recruited by anybody. I had no idea what I was going to do with my life. Let the bastards cruise; *I* wasn't going to jump aboard ship for any of them.

And I had a sudden premonition that it would be the worst decision of Phil's life if he did jump on board.

I think it's safe to say that the summer of 1953 was a memorable time for most Americans. Back on July 27, the so-called non-war in Korea had come to an end at the hand of our new president, Dwight D. Eisenhower.

Talk about spared lives. After more than 50,000 American deaths and countless more Koreans, North and South, the madness was finally over, or at least on hold. We no longer had to worry about the fulfillment of our ROTC obligation after graduation; we would serve out our commitment in relative safety. And surely, we all agreed, our country would never again engage in such an unnecessary venture of military commitment. We had a leader now who understood the insanity of war from personal experience. We could count on Ike to keep us safe, free, and clear-headed.

****

I suppose it is ironic that in spite of all the new and suspect acquaintances that I was acquiring in New Orleans, along with the questionable horde left over from the Tampa Bay area, that I had begun to consider the possibility of the FBI as a career choice.

Another friend and non-scholarship schoolmate from Tampa, Bill Ferlita, was employed in the New Orleans FBI field office headquarters as a night clerk while working his way through school and had begun to encourage me.

I spent many nighttime hours at the FBI office near Lee Circle on St. Charles Avenue and found myself being drawn into the Bureau orbit. I'd learned that the Bureau's hands-off relationship with Carlos Marcello was grounded in a "private understanding" of some sort between New York crime lord Frank Costello and Hoover.

"After Lucky Luciano was imprisoned," Billy explained late one night over a plate of bacon and scrambled eggs, "Costello had become head of the major crime family in New York City and by 1940 was thought to be the premier *Mafiosi* in America." He laughed. "At least in the estimation of those who believed in the existence of a Mafia."

The waiter refilled our coffee cups, and a man stumbled in and sat next to us at the counter. Billy turned to me and lowered his voice.

"Costello was a good friend and colleague of Carlos Marcello. When a reform ticket in New York City forced Costello out of his gambling operation — not all of his interests, mind you — he came south." He lit a cigarette and courteously blew smoke away from me. "By this time, Marcello had begun to establish himself as the successor to old Sam Carolla, whom the government had recently deported. Now, along with Meyer Lansky as a third partner, Costello and Carlos established the Beverly Country Club, a lavish casino operation in nearby Jefferson Parish named after Marcello's mother."

Billy sipped his coffee and drew deeply on his cigarette, and I said wryly, "Of course the club was able to function entirely without police interference."

He grinned through the smoke haze. "This is New Orleans, Georgie."

"What about the local FBI? They can't be deaf, dumb and blind."

He paid the check and got up. At the door he laughed and said, "You remember the local SAC's testimony at the Kefauver hearings — Marcello, he said under oath, was a legitimate real estate investor and a dealer in tomato paste!" He was laughing hard as we stepped onto the sidewalk. "Hoover's continued position is that there is no such thing as the Mafia. And even though I shouldn't be saying all of this to an outsider, I have to talk to someone or blow my stack."

"Go ahead, I won't tell."

"Well, you never know who's a spy around this place. I keep my mouth shut and my eyes and ears open; you'd be surprised what you can learn that way." We started walking. "I like most of the street agents, they're great guys. The suits are the pains in the ass, always trying to catch the street workers in some kind of fuck-up, anything that will look good on their own résumés Believe me, the night shift I work is a good time to get an ear-full."

"Like what? What are you ..."

"Like maybe Hoover's on the take," he suddenly blurted.

"What!" I came to a sudden halt. "What the hell are you saying, man? J. Edgar Hoover? Why, he's the greatest ..."

He turned back to me and said, "Look, I'm only saying what I hear, Georgie. And not all of them agree. But is the old man's reluctance to go after the mob based on ignorance or mob leverage?"

"What kind of leverage?"

"I don't know for sure. Sexual or gambling dirt."

"Jesus, you hear what you're saying?"

"Rumor is Costello and Lansky have documents."

I must have looked sick.

"It's not just me; everybody talks about what a gambler he is. He loves betting on the horses. He frequents all the major race tracks in the country, see, and always as the guest of one gangster or corrupt businessman or another. The Texas oil barons, Sid Richardson and Clint Murchison, are his largest sponsors. And one thing is certain: the Hoov's the only track addict in America who's never held a losing ticket."

The streetcar came clattering along the tracks and stopped long enough for us to dash across the avenue and hop aboard. We popped in our tokens and settled on seats half-way along the nearly empty car. "You ever hear of Paul Montrose?"

"Doctor Montrose, the sociologist over at Tulane? Sure. I even read one of his books on the ongoing failures of man."

"He's said to be a genius and an authority on criminology and crime in America. He's also light in the loafers and friends of that Shaw fellow, you know the one. Throws all those risqué parties at his place down in the Quarter. And if you haven't already attended one, then my advice is to stay the hell away."

"That's what I've heard."

He laughed, but it wasn't a mirthful sound. "I run into Montrose now and again at one of his favorite drinking holes in the Quarter.

He lowered his voice in spite of the near-emptiness of the carriage. "One night in the bar at Pat O'Brien's, he was running his mouth like he had a case of verbal diarrhea, and when he learned from one of our tablemates that I clerked for the Bureau, he really cut loose. Started in on how Hoover and everyone around him is queer. Claimed to have seen photos of Hoover and Tolson captured en *flagrante delicto,* as he put it. You know how they live, bachelors, as close as most married couples. It seems to support the rumors. According to Montrose, it's documentation like this that's kept Hoover in line over the years. The mob has got the goods on him, and he knows they'll use it."

Hoover and Clyde Tolson

"I feel sick at my stomach. The way I've idealized that man all of my life."

But one look at Billy told me there was more of the same on the way.

"Now get ready, old buddy, and hold on to your seat. Montrose said — and he's got great contacts, you know, been teaching criminology here and about for a hundred years — he said

Hoover was arrested some years ago on a French Quarter morals charge. A charge that was promptly squelched by Marcello's control of the coppers downtown."

I was genuinely shocked by such revelations and by the fact that we were even having such a conversation. Somehow what we were talking about was probably illegal, and it was damned sure un-American.

"Well, I've shot my mouth off enough for one night, and I'm not even drunk. What I've said though might get me killed if you run your mouth in the wrong places. It'll damned sure get me fired." He looked out the window, jumped to his feet and yelped: "Here's our stop!"

We bounced off the streetcar and ran across the avenue toward the campus. Billy lived in an apartment nearby and got rid of me at the Ranch House.

I sat alone on the porch unable to turn off the confusion in my mind. I rehashed all that had been said and tried to come to terms with the astonishing conclusion that monopolized my thoughts. But whatever the truth was behind Hoover's forbearance in the face of the obvious existence of organized crime in most of the major cities throughout the nation, the city of New Orleans was so wide open that most tourists simply believed that gambling, drugs and prostitution were all legal in the state of Louisiana.

One night in the Quarter late in the wet-cold of February, Angelique Trepanier and I were on our way through Jackson Square and over to the Café du Monde when a voice rang out behind us.

"Hey, kid, it's good t'see you again!"

It was David Ferrie, dressed in an outfit that Robin Hood might have worn in the forest deep. But Ferrie was no Errol Flynn.

To accommodate the rare skin disease that was inexorably rendering his body hairless from head to toe, he swept what little head-hair he still retained over the spreading bald spot on his crown and fluffed the front up above his forehead like a pile of dried seaweed. He would be forced into a toupée in the near future. He already wore thick pasted-on eyebrows that produced a Bozo-the-Clown look sufficiently garish to frighten little children.

He handed me a business card with his address and the name Banister on it and said, "I want you to come around and see us, okay? You can help us, and we can be of help to you. Gimme a call, soon. I gotta go now. Call me."

And he was gone.

"You *know* that creep?" Angelique said in a shocked, accusatory tone as we crossed over to the crowded café and secured a fresh-air table. I'd been dating her for a couple of weeks.

"I've seen him around a couple of times. I don't *know* him, certainly not in the Biblical sense."

"My father says he's queer, crooked, and crazy as a loon," she said as a waiter took our orders for Creole coffee and a platter of the world-famous powdered beignets.

"He's hooked up with all the perverts and gangsters in the Quarter, says my friend Mary Elizabeth. She dates Jim Garrison in the D.A.'s office and says Jim knows just about everything there is to know in this town about everything. Whatever *that* means."

"Means he's a good guy to know, if it's true."

Our coffee and doughnuts were served steaming hot and we dug in. It was difficult to enjoy our late night treat, however, due to my jumbled thoughts. Hell, I knew some things too, as a result of my talk during summer vacation with Phil Agee and recently with Bill Ferlita and Frank Klein, and the earlier meeting with Ferrie to which he had eluded. It hadn't been of much concern to me at the time, but now, after all I'd learned lately, I was beginning to suspect that many of these people were somehow connected.

I'd first encountered Ferrie when a classmate persuaded me to attend a meeting of the Civil Air Patrol one night out at Lake Pontchartrain. The food and drink were good, and there were guys I already knew. Boogie Murret's young cousin Lee was there. He and his divorced mother lived with the Murret family. His full name was Lee Harvey Oswald. I would often see him around, but we had no meaningful contact.

Need I say that I wasn't moved to sign up with the Patrol in spite of the patriotic hurrah issued by the primary speaker of the evening, a commander of one of the local CAP (patrol) units? "It is the duty of every good American to serve the nation in its time of need." Dave Ferrie had railed from the podium, having spoken for some twenty or thirty minutes non-stop. In spite of the eccentric appearance that was just beginning to show, he was an articulate and effective spokesman for his provocative agenda.

He made an impassioned plea for patriotic recruits to the CAP cause of preparedness. "And make no mistake about it, my friends, *this* is such a time. The Communist threat is real. They intend to bury us. We can hear the sabers rattling, if only we will open our ears."

Tall and lean with a protruding belly, he was a dynamic speaker, well-educated and talented and not yet incapacitated by his loathsome skin disease, known as *alopecia praecox*. And in spite of his reputation as a first-class pilot, he would soon be fired by Eastern Airlines as a result of a series of homosexual exploits with young boys. He would then become a private investigator in the employ of Carlos Marcello.

In my circle, however bright and talented he might be, he was considered a foul-mouthed buffoon of psychotic proportions and was given a wide berth. Although I ran into him a number of times thereafter in the Quarter, I always maintained a wary distance. After the Patrol meeting that night, he left the lakefront with Lee Oswald and two other young protégés.

Guy Banister was another piece of work to remember. A twenty-year veteran of the FBI who had supervised the capture of John Dillinger, he'd worked during the war with OSS and Naval Intelligence and was finally forced into retirement from the Bureau for excessive drinking. Having been born and raised in Louisiana, he came home to New Orleans in the '50s and signed on as a deputy chief of police. He lasted in this position until 1957 when he was dismissed from the force after threatening a waiter with a gun in an alcohol-induced public frenzy.

In appearance, Banister was an immaculately dressed man who wore tailored suits with fresh flowers in the lapels. He had neat, close-cropped hair and electric blue eyes. But belying his dapper, somewhat professorial image, he was a modern-day Neanderthal. A cunning alcoholic with a mercurial temper and the personality of a pit viper, he was a visceral racist who hated blacks, Jews and Communists almost as much as he hated Chief Justice

Earl Warren and the U.S. Supreme Court for what he labeled their recent despotic ruling in Brown v. Board of Education.

Even while Rosa Parks was taking her Alabama bus ride into history, Banister was running a network of young informants who spied for him in local schools and colleges throughout the city and state. They reported on instances of subversive activity and signs of racial free-thinking among faculty and student body. Of course, none of his youthful sleuths had any idea what he proposed to do with such information beyond the compilation of his lists.

Through no effort of my own I had numerous sessions with him in a variety of hot spots throughout the French Quarter. He seemed to like me and always bought me a beer and a pizza or hoagie, and he was always — no matter how drunk — wrapped in his patriotic banner.

"The Commies are comin' and your kind better watch your backsides. And the niggers" — he always had a few choice words of vitriol regarding the white man's burden — "too goddamn stupid to know what's good for 'em. But it's the Commies got 'em all stirred up. Soon gonna send 'em out into the streets burning, looting and raping."

The litany never changed. But in all of these conversations he never sought to steer me toward the FBI as a career choice. In his cups, he loved to tell about the days of shoot -'em-ups with the likes of Dillinger and Pretty Boy Floyd. But he always encouraged me toward work with an intelligence agency such as NIA, CIA, or the Army's counter-intelligence service. I could hear echoes of *"Marteen"* running *his* case at me.

One night in one of our favorite hangouts on Tchoupitoulas Street, after three or four Chivas Regals straight, Banister really opened up. "That recent brouhaha down in Guatemala was just a warm-up, see. That fuckin' Arias wasn't a pimple on a real dictator's ass, but he was a bona fide nationalizing Commie, and he had to go."

He became drunker and louder with every refill. "It's VP Nixon, y'know. He was the one who spearheaded the Guatemalan coup when that little wop tried to take over the assets of the National Fruit Company. Nixon and the Dulles brothers. And now if Ike'll just drop dead from another of those heart attacks, we'll have us a real Red-hater in the White House. Then with Nixon we can raise some hell all over the Caribbean."

"Maybe we can even get rid of Batista down there in Cuba," I said, intentionally provocative.

Banister's bright blue eyes blazed with irritation. "You being a smart ass, or what? Batista's no Commie; he's a man we can do business with. We have for a long time now and that's the way we're gonna keep it."

"What about all those Cubans who want him out?"

He laughed an ugly sound and signaled the waiter for another shot. "You mean that goddamn fool Castro-oil? Guy who recently led the attack on the Moncado Barracks? Asshole's in prison."

"I heard he's been released and is on his way into the mountains."

"Shoulda just shot the Commie prick and been done with it." He took a big slug of the whisky and then glared across the table at me. "You seem to think you know a lot about what's going on in Cuba."

I shrugged. "I have a lot of friends from Cuba. They and their families don't think Castro's such a joke."

"Well, I hope they won't be too disappointed when Batista has his balls boiled in oil in the Presidential Square."

"I don't know, my friends say ..." but that was as far as I got.

"Hey! I'm tired of hearing from your goddamned friends, and I'm damned tired of hearing from you!"

Banister had literally ignited. His face was boil-red, his eyes febrile lights of fury, and he'd come across the table in a menacing posture that had me reacting instinctively.

"Get out of my face, man."

Patrons were gawking, alert to potential violence. Some of them knew him.

"Out of your face? Up your sweet ass," he snarled and shoved the table against my chest. I shoved back and tried to stand as a team of burly waiters arrived and quelled the disturbance before it got out of hand. They knew Banister and his reputation well.

"Okay, okay, mind the suit. Mind the fuckin' suit!" he bellowed.

Our glasses had been overturned in the shoving match, and some of the whisky now spotted his jacket. It took some moments to right the disorder and to get Banister and the nearby guests resettled at their booths and tables. Banister tossed back still another shot of whisky and said to me as if absolutely nothing untoward had occurred: "Now look, kid. Let me tell you how you can help the cause and do yourself some good in the bargain."

But at least he paid the bill and staggered off in the direction of Canal Street, and I wandered over toward Bourbon in search of a more agreeable atmosphere. God help the good citizens of New Orleans, I thought, with *that* guy serving as one of its top cops.

It was only a week or so later that Sonia Bascom, a friend of mine from the night, laid a big one on me. I'd been seeing her often in recent weeks and at first was terrified that her news bulletin was that she'd recently come up pregnant. But that wasn't it. Still, she gave it to me between the eyes, and I left her apartment that evening a sadder but wiser young man.

We'd gone for a river boat ride, dined at *Café Du Monde* and strolled most every street in the Quarter. Then we'd had sex upstairs in her garden apartment. The radio was playing "Wheel of Fortune" when she told me that she was leaving New Orleans the next day and going home to Texas. She had a good job offer and couldn't say no.

"I'm going to Dallas," she said, nervously twisting a pearl teardrop around her neck, "to dance at one of Jack Ruby's clubs. It's a good deal that I just couldn't turn down. He promised me a featured act, more prestige, and a whole lot more money."

"Jack Ruby," I groused, shocked by the sudden announcement. "He's the guy who got arrested for murder last year over there in Dallas."

"Jack gets arrested a lot of times on a variety of charges. Nothing ever sticks."

"He's a bad actor, Sonia. Used to run guns and drugs down in Tampa during the war. You shouldn't want to have anything to do with a guy like him."

"Well, like I said, I can't say no."

"Won't he get in trouble, stealing you away from one of Marcello's clubs here?"

She smiled. "Jack works for the boys, silly. He does what he's told."

"And you — do you always do what you're told?"

Her expression froze momentarily, then she shrugged it off. "I told you, Georgie. It's a good opportunity for me, a real chance to be noticed." She raised her shoulders and jutted her chin. "I may not be much of an actress yet, but I look good enough to make it in the movies, or at least on TV."

"I don't think whoring for gangsters is the best way to go about a movie career," I said callously, and Sonia grimaced as if I'd slapped her. Her face flushed and her eyes filled with tears, but before I could apologize she was off the bed and stationed by the window overlooking the courtyard.

I followed and wrapped her in my arms. She accepted my embrace and silent apology and then softened as I kissed her behind the ear.

"Stinker," she said.

"It was a rotten thing to say. It's just that I ..."

"I know how you feel about it. Maybe ... maybe if I'd met you earlier ... but it's too late for anything like that." She turned in my arms and kissed me. "Now it's on to Dallas and then Hollywood and stardom."

****

The new semesters were upon us. And it was in this period, 1954–55, that I began to have contact with a number of important characters that were destined to play significant roles on the national scene in the very near future.

One night after one of my aimless rambles in the Quarter, I stopped in at Felix's Oyster Bar and Restaurant on Bourbon Street. The bistro was owned by Sam Saia, overseer of Carlos Marcello's gambling network. I would learn a good deal more about this operation in the coming weeks and months. But on this particular night I was hunkered down at a corner table over a plate of raw oysters when I was suddenly joined by none other than my old nemesis Martin. Without preamble he sat down, ordered a dozen oysters and a schooner of beer, and started in on me.

"Been a long time, kid, but I been watching you."

He blathered on for awhile, and I waited him out. Beer and oysters kept coming and then he spun a story that was worth waiting for. He'd spent the recent past in a part of the world that I and most Americans knew little about. A place that was now being called Vietnam, way off over in Indo-China.

"The Frogs got their butts kicked in Dien Bien Phu. Now it's all ours for the taking. We're in the process of establishing something you've never heard of, the Saigon Military Mission, or SMM. It's not military; it's *our* operation, *my* guys; SMM's a Company cover. I went over with checkbook in hand to establish a nation."

He laughed as if he'd said something hilarious, something significant, and it would be a long time in the future before I realized that he had indeed done so. He'd signaled for me the start of a twenty-year U.S. involvement in that part of the world that would cost us more than 58,000 American boys and many hundreds of billions of dollars, coupled with millions of lost Vietnamese, all wasted lives and money.

Martin sucked down an oyster and licked the shell dry. "Okay, you want to know why I'm telling you such things. Things that could get me shot if you were to run your mouth. Well, I'm trying to give you a head's up. Prepare you for what's coming. I still think you've got a bright future, and I want to help you."

"Why the hell should you want to help me?"

"That's for me to know and you to find out when the time is right."

He looked up and signaled to a man who had just entered the bar. This guy was gray-haired, impeccably dressed and walked with a noticeable limp. I recognized him from occasional sightings around the Quarter. He limped over to our table and sat down, and I had the queasy feeling that the meeting was not accidental.

"Clay Bertrand," Martin said as he sucked the juice from another oyster shell, "meet George Mettler."

Bertrand shook my hand across the table. "Pleased to meet you, I've heard a lot about you. Basketball at Loyola, right? I don't see many ballgames." Then he said, "I hear you're considering government service."

I looked balefully at Martin. "Where did you hear that?"

Bertrand ignored my response. "There are many opportunities today for a young man with your fine qualifications." I didn't bother to ask what he knew of my qualifications, fine or otherwise, and he said, "I know people, and it's just possible that I can be of help to you, so let's stay in touch. I live here in the Quarter, over on Dauphine Street. I'll have you over some night for a quality meal and a good talk."

He stood up, actually bowed, then nodded to us both and limped away.

I glared across the table at Martin. "Now what the hell was *that* all about?"

"Your life and wellbeing," he said and signaled the waiter for our bill.

Martin paid my tab too, and we went our separate ways into the night. I stood for a moment on Bourbon Street, uncertain what to do or think about all that had just transpired. Then I decided to hell with it, that none of this fog and smoke had anything to do with me, and I walked around the corner to Preservation Hall.

A few nights later Frank Klein came by the Ranch House and invited me to take a walk with him. I liked Frank and was intrigued by what I knew about him, so I didn't even hesitate. We didn't walk far, stopping at one of the benches alongside Marquette Hall on campus. We sat down, and with no preliminaries Frank said, "I happened to see you the other night in the Quarter. You were eating and drinking at the Oyster Bar with a guy I know only by reputation and your friend with the limp."

"Clay Bertrand," I said. "But he's not my friend; I never exchanged a word with him prior to that night."

"And the other guy?"

"Don't really know him either."

"Goes by the name of Martin some of the time. He's a bad actor, so be careful."

I felt gaseous jets of acidic concern bubbling up in my blood. What the hell was *this* all about?

"Bertrand's real name is Shaw," Frank continued. "Clay Shaw, Director of the New Orleans International Trade Mart. Watch out for him too, especially if he invites you to his house for a cozy dinner."

"He already has."

"Be on your guard, he's bent as a broken bicycle spoke."

Then he decided to tell me what was really on his mind.

"Look, they're all in cahoots one way or another. Martin is CIA, up to his eyeballs in slime. Shaw was OSS during the war and afterwards worked in Italy for many years and is clearly tied in today with the mob and the Agency. They'll suck you into it all, if they possibly can. Recruiting is a big thing with those guys. Merit badges for every recruit they succeed in bringing on board. Don't listen to them, George."

We walked back over to the Ranch House and at the back steps Frank tapped me on the shoulder and said, "Let's keep in touch. Got to be careful these days who we talk to, the Commie hunters are gearing up more than ever, and we're in for some bad times."

Jim Garrison soon became district attorney in New Orleans and was the only law official in the country to prosecute anyone for the assassination of President Kennedy. His target was Clay Shaw, aka Clay Bertrand, and David Ferrie. Garrison's

Clay Shaw

chief legal assistant in that day was Frank Klein. But all of this came in a future time.

Frank was right with his prognostication that night. The year brought profound changes in the nation's life as well as in our personal lives. The Middle East was in turmoil. Nationalist China and Communist forces were fighting over the offshore islands of Quemoy and Matsu, and in a place called South Vietnam the

French struggle for continued colonial power in Indo-china had collapsed after a final disastrous battle loss at Dien Bien Phu. South Vietnam promptly christened itself a Republic.

As I understood it, Vietnam was now two countries, North and South, and I thought I smelled chaos over there in the near future, especially after what Martin had told me about the CIA's Saigon Military Mission. I suspected U.S. fingerprints were all over present-day events in that region of the world. I'd tried to learn more at the library, but the SMM was flying almost entirely under the radar.

Closer to home shores, Argentina's Peron was forced out of office in a coup said to have been instigated by the CIA, while the same bunch of covert operators were thought to have been responsible for the assassination of the president of Panama. There seemed to be no end to what our government would do in the name of democracy.

Meanwhile the U.S. Senate extended the investigations of domestic Communism, and thousands of federal employees were dismissed as so-called security risks, and a black man named Martin Luther King led a boycott of the segregated bus lines in Montgomery, Alabama.

Here in New Orleans, we almost had our own homemade race riots when it was announced that Loyola was scheduled to play a team in our home gymnasium that included two blacks in the starting lineup. Never mind the fact that they were two of the finest basketball players ever to lace up their gym shoes, Bill Russell and K. C. Jones. But the media knew a good story and incited the whole state onto the edge of a conniption fit.

But the semester ended without a conflagration, Galvin and most of the Chicago crowd graduated, and the rest of us spread out in various directions for summer vacation.

＊＊＊＊＊＊＊＊＊＊＊＊＊＊

The Ranch House was like alien territory come the following semester, and I had to learn my way around all over again. There were new boys from Michigan, New Mexico,

Oklahoma and New York. All the outrageous hijinks of yesteryear were adventures of the past.

One night I was walking along Canal Street on my way to the Lowe's Estate Theatre to see the new Humphrey Bogart movie, and a car suddenly honked and pulled to the curb alongside me. The back window rolled down and Santo Jr. said, "Get in, Georgie. Come take a ride."

I hadn't seen him in quite some time. I slid into the seat next to him, we shook hands and then Santo caressed my face with warmth and sincere good will. As always, he was kind and gracious and exuded an instinctive old-world charm that was most appealing. "It is good to see you, my friend. Why are you not studying?"

"It's good to see you, too. And a good student is not all work and no play. Besides, I am doing research for a sociology term paper that's due next week."

He laughed affably. "We go over to Antoinne's, and you will continue your research." He nodded to his driver and away we went. "You were in Tampa and did not come to see me."

I wasn't surprised that he knew of my comings and goings, since he knew most everything that went on in Tampa. I apologized and said that I didn't want to impose.

"You could have come to Havana as my guest."

That would have been quite a treat as Santo Jr. was the Man now.

"I was sorry to hear about your father."

"It was a good thing you did, sending your card of sympathy."

I'd had no idea whether he'd seen it or not. "Cuba," I asked. "Is it safe?"

He shrugged. "Not exactly safe. But we have important business interests there that must be attended to."

"What about Castro?"

Another shrug. "The belief is that Batista will crush him."

"What do you think, if I may ask?"

"Such belief may be wrong."

I couldn't help wishing there could be a round table discussion on the subject between Santo, Guy Banister, Clay Shaw and David Ferrie with me monitoring the proceeding from off-stage. We cruised up to the entrance of the historic restaurant, and a uniformed attendant began opening doors with a flourish. Another attendant escorted us past the knot of impatiently waiting diners without a moment's hesitation.

We went to the bar and had a drink. Santo had brandy and I had a gin and tonic. When our waiter stopped to ask if we cared for another round on the house, Santo shook him off and said, "I wish we could visit at our leisure, but I have a pressing engagement."

He gestured to me with his glass and said, *"Salud."* Then he stood and caressed my neck and shoulders and said, "Come, I will walk you out."

As we passed an open door to one of the private rooms, Santo stopped. "A moment, Georgie. You wait."

I moved to a better vantage point to see inside. The large room was decorated in muted reds and beiges with a colorful mural in bright blues and yellows on the far wall. A long banquet table was arranged in horseshoe fashion, and a side table on wheels bore the largest antipasto I'd ever seen. A special cadre of waiters bustled in and out of the room and hovered around the table. I'd never seen so much food for so few prospective diners. Perhaps they were going to feed the multitude after their repast.

Five or six guests mingled in amiable conversation, all men, and others were still arriving. I noticed a priest, not someone that I recognized from the university, and a well-known politician on the city council. Anthony Marcello caught my eye and waved, and standing near the mural in a cluster of well-dressed men was Carlos Marcello.

He wore a dark tailored suit with a pearl white vest, shirt and tie. I watched, fascinated, as each man who approached the old lion bowed and reached for his hand, not to shake it, but rather to raise it to their lips in a gesture of respect and obeisance. Santo approached and whispered into his host's ear. Marcello looked over at me, nodded, and Santo returned to me and took me by the arm.

"Don Carlos, this is George Mettler, a friend of mine from Tampa. A fine athlete and a boy of promise, he was a special favorite of my father."

"Greetings," Marcello said. "It's good t'see you again. I see ya over by da motel some udder nights. You college boys like t'play more dan you study." He spoke pigeon English with a heavy accent basted in virgin olive oil.

The men in the group laughed dutifully, Santo smiled, and I said, "We didn't know anything about fun until we came to New Orleans."

More laughter and Marcello said, "Let da good times roll, hey!"

Santo and I stepped aside as another acolyte drew near, reached for the don's hand and raised it respectfully to his lips. Santo walked me into the crowded foyer.

"You be good," he said. "Study hard, make your mother and all of us proud. And remember, you need anything, you call Anthony."

We shook hands and Santo drew me into an old-world *abrazo* and kissed me warmly on both cheeks.

"Hey, Margaret, did'ja see *that?*" bellowed a man in green polyester trousers and a yellow sport coat standing in the tourist line as Santo turned back inside and I started for the exit.

I stopped, looked at the startled couple and smiled cheerfully. "That's the way it is in New Orleans, buddy. Tell him, Margaret. *Laissez les bon temps rouler.*"

"Say *what!*" the man demanded as I pushed on through the door.

One day at practice before the season had even begun, I dribbled in for a layup, made the basket, and landed awkwardly. I couldn't get up unaided, couldn't walk for days. My playing season was over before it had begun. The diagnosis: a ruptured disc. Basketball was off the charts for me, and the weakness in my spine has plagued me all of my life.

One afternoon, I limped out of the field house and bumped into Boogie Murret's young cousin, Lee Harvey Oswald. "It's almost over. He'll be out soon."

"Don't matter none," he said. "I got nothin' else to do."

The boy was an odd duck. I'd talked with him a couple of times at David Ferrie's CAP meetings but never spent much time with him. I knew he had grown up in his uncle's home but had only limited knowledge of the Murret family.

Of course, I knew Boogie, my teammate, but I was a couple of years ahead of him, and we weren't close. From newspapers, I'd learned that Dutz Murret worked for Carlos Marcello and that Lee's mother dated men from the Marcello *borgata*. Besides his cousin Boogie, there was another cousin who was a Catholic priest and an older Murret daughter, an attractive young woman who was an inveterate world traveler and was widely rumored to be some sort of CIA agent or asset.

It was an interesting family. Lee Harvey Oswald grew up to become the government-designated lone assassin of the President of the United States.

A Man of Honor

PART SIX

Law and Disorder

Springfield, Illinois, 1961

"One or two, okay, but how the hell did you develop relationships with so many significant characters. I never knew even one guy like that back in my day."

"You never lived in Tampa or New Orleans," I laughed.

"And how did you get past the first stage of our applicant investigation?"

"Nobody cared. You remember what training school was like, organized crime was hardly mentioned. The word Mafia was an obscenity. J. Edgar told the world that the Mafia didn't exist, and no instructor was going to contradict the master's word. Hell, I knew more about the Mafia than any of our instructors."

I was lunching with Phil Agee late in July. We both wore jeans and flowered sport shirts in the Joe College fashion of the day. We'd talked on the phone a couple of times and had lunch twice. It was an odd relationship, but we had a lot in common beyond our high school experience at Jesuit and four years each at Catholic universities. We were both discontented in Tampa, but for different reasons. Even with Phil, I wouldn't discuss my reasons. I wanted more experience to write about. He was agonizing over career considerations too. "I don't think I could have made it in South Bend much longer. And I don't know if I want to come back to Tampa to stay."

"What about the family business? Your mother's counting on you."

"That's what makes it so rough on me. After Dad died — I feel so damned guilty. It's been a family affair for generations, and I don't want to jump ship without a good reason."

"Well, what's your reason? What's your alternative?"

"Law school."

"What? Another damned lawyer! I thought you had more ambition than that."

He laughed as the waitress refilled our iced tea glasses.

"What does Martin have to say about this?"

Phil shrugged. "He sees it as a three-year delay, but says he's sure I'll then come on board. Says that after law school, the

Company has a way for me to serve two years in the military as a cover in some sort of off-the-books arrangement. And then when my two years are up, I'll enter the JOT — the Junior Officer Training Program in Washington — on my way to becoming a career case officer."

"I already have a commission and will be an officer and a gentleman on the day I report for active duty."

"That's why they're so interested in you. Or would be, if you would give them the time of day."

"I'll think about it."

"Think hard, George. At least talk with them."

Shortly thereafter, Phil moved to Gainesville and enrolled in the University of Florida law school. I moved up to Georgia with Mama into snug quarters in the old family farmhouse and enrolled in the Walter F. George School of Law at Mercer University in nearby Macon.

I was moving in a hot miasma of self-deception.

****

I now reasoned that if I possessed a law degree, I would be a viable candidate for the FBI. At last, in reality, not just in childish imagination, a G-man! It was mind-boggling, but my Tampa friend in New Orleans, Bill Ferlita, had convinced me that it was a distinct possibility.

So law school would be the first step. Then once I was in fact a bona-fide G-man with all of that inside information enhanced by personal experiences that even most G-men didn't possess, I would begin to tell my stories. Mickey Spillane, Graham Greene, John LeCarre — forget about it.

Well, Blackstone Legal Books, here I come! I enrolled in Mercer University in Macon, Georgia.

In late July, before school cranked up for my second year, doctors informed our family that my mother was not well and required a warmer climate and healthier living environment. I agreed to take her home and to transfer to Stetson College of Law across the Bay from Tampa. And since school wouldn't begin until

September of that year, 1957, I had time on my hands. I got to work and made plans for the next great adventure of my life: Cuba.

Mr. San Marco had previously introduced me to the Cuesta brothers, José and Pepé, Cubans who had operated a charter fishing company along Key West, the Cayman Islands and Cuba. José was in his mid-forties, Pepé about ten years younger. Pepé was short and pudgy, José tall and well built.

We had a stopover in Grand Cayman on our way to Cuba. At the far end of the broad sloping street was the harbor with the sea drawn calm and shining like a mirror in the hard bright sun. But what struck me most emphatically was not a matter of sight at all but rather one of smell: the unmistakable smell of the tropics. The hot, dark, mysterious scent of Africa, and the exotic, spicy and pungent aroma of the Orient. All of it rising out of that baking dry dust of the ages like a monument, pervading, insinuating. It was the kiss of Africa upon your quivering lips, an Oriental whisper of antiquity against the hot sensitive ear.

"We gonna have to kill the *barbudos*," Pepé suddenly blurted. "Eef not today, then tomorrow or the next day. I hope you will be on our side, mon."

I was jarred by Pepe's sudden segue into the here and now as we stopped at a harbor hotel. We'd heard that Castro had left Mexico City and was probably already back in Cuba. I wondered if I might see him during my visit.

Havana was amazing but would be difficult to assimilate in such a brief encounter as was planned for me. All my advisors were right enough; this was not a good time for such a visit. I was troubled by the wretched social conditions that prevailed in this so-called Paris of the Antilles.

But change was in the air. You could feel it all around you, smell it in the breeze off the sea and the winds gusting down from the mountains. And Fidel Castro was leading the charge. The government had been caught in a white-hot lie when it put out a bulletin that Fidel had been located and killed in the mountains by Batista's military police. An article documenting the lie was published in the New York Times, and the genie was out of the bottle. Cuba would soon be of interest to the world for reasons other than gambling sorties and smutty getaways.

I decided to stay away from Santo's Hotel Capri, where actor George Raft served as the greeter. I was here to see and learn. I had a small room for sleeping in Central Havana across the Paseo and alongside the Old Presidential Palace, and all of Havana lay at my disposal for everything else. Within the hour, I was unpacked and back out on the street.

The city was a symphony of sound and movement. American cars of the fifties, well-preserved and battered, crowded the streets. Sidewalks roiled with armed Cuban soldiers and police, garishly-dressed tourists, and uniformed U.S. sailors on shore leave. Prostitutes of every age, color and gender worked the pedestrian throng.

Without doubt, the highlight of my island visit was the meeting with Alicia Valez, Artice's sixteen-year-old daughter. My original sponsor, now Father San Marco, and Artice Valez were distant cousins, as I remember it, one raised in Cuba, the other in America, and they had visited back and forth with each other all through the years. Valez was not a wealthy man; he was not a landowner or business tycoon. I think he was a pharmacist, what in America would be called a successful member of the middle class.

His daughter was one of the loveliest girls I'd ever met.

"I am pleased to make your acquaintance," she said in correct convent English as we sat in the living room of their comfortable apartment with a striking view of the vast Atlantic beyond the Malécon.

"It was nice of your father to invite me," I said, glancing around the simple but elegantly furnished room. There was a fireplace with a lovely gilt-framed mirror over the mantle that allowed me to look at Alicia from varying vantage points.

"Any friend of Father San Marco is a friend of the Valez family," she said, and as she moved to refill my glass with ice-cold lemonade I thought I might swoon. She moved with the grace of a ballet dancer. Her skin was dark and smooth, her eyes as shiny-black as moist olives, her sleek hair artfully groomed in a ponytail that reached nearly to her waist. And her scent, well, it simply took my breath away.

"Have you been to the states?"

"I have never been anywhere." Her tone and manner held less regret than anticipation. "But I will go to America someday, and I too will attend college. I will learn much about your country and the ways of the world, and then I will come home ..."

"You won't come back," I laughed. "You'll get married, have five children and make a home of your own."

She didn't even smile. "You are wrong, Jorge. I will most certainly come back to Cuba. To a free Cuba in which ..."

The front door opened and her father arrived. *"Hola, nina! Y Jorge, bienvenido!"*

Alicia jumped to her feet and met him with a warm embrace. He kissed her cheeks and lifted her momentarily off her feet in a gesture that filled me with envy. I stood and shook hands with my host and was surprised again by how tall he was. It seemed that most Cubans were under six feet and either overweight or muscular.

"I will just go in and see how Mama is progressing with the meal, and then we will dine and you will tell us all the news concerning the political situation in your country. Will Nixon truly be your next president?"

We had a wonderful lunch of raw oysters, vegetables and deep fried flounder. Valez was an attentive host, his wife Consuela a gracious woman, and their daughter a continuing wonder to behold. Over coffee and cake the conversation turned serious.

"I am always warning Americans about visiting in our country. The time is not right. You must not linger, Jorge. I have already spoken with José and Pepé. They will be ready to sail on the morning tide."

I bolted upright, but he allowed me no time to question his decision. Alicia sat with hands folded, eyes down, and her mother cleared the table. When Alicia made as if to rise and help, her mother said, "No. You stay. Listen and learn."

"We are facing big trouble in Cuba, and it must be confronted. You are aware that Fidel has returned from Mexico City and is encamped in the mountains with his small band of rebel fighters. Violence is erupting all over the island." I could see it. Cuba and the Havana mob were being remade. And Valez said that the spirit of revolution had boiled over and would soon arrive in Havana.

Alicia brought a pot of fresh coffee and resumed her seat without uttering a word. It was all stunning; we'd heard little of this back home, and no one cared in any case. Cuba's world was turning inside out and the world of the mob with it. So what the hell was *I* doing here? I looked at Artice, then at Alicia. In her silence she had not missed a word. Was she even serving as one of the terrorists; packing explosives, delivering supplies after school? I was never to learn the answer to such questions.

"Now you must go, Jorge," Alicia said.

We were startled by Alicia's sudden interjection, the only words she had uttered during our conversation. Her mouth was set, her limpid eyes wide with determination.

"*Si,*" her father said, "in the morning without delay."

The return adventure began at dawn. Both my eyelids and my heart were heavy. Pepé waited for me in front of the rooming house, loaded my bags and off we went.

* * * * * * * * * * * * *

The law school at Stetson was situated on the Gulf beach near St. Petersburg. I commuted each day from our new residence on Aquilla Street in the Palma Ceia section of Tampa. The old stucco and tile facility resembled a country club rather than a law school.

I had drinks one afternoon in downtown Tampa with Frank Ragano, an old hand out of Ybor City. In the near future, Frank would develop an interesting clientele in the criminal field with a list that would include Santo Trafficante, Carlos Marcello and Jimmy Hoffa.

Martin popped up one morning and took me to Malio's on Dale Mabry Avenue for lunch. It was a wiseguy hangout, and I would have preferred somewhere else, but Martin wasn't concerned. In fact, he seemed to be acquainted with many of these people.

"Why are you doing this?"

"Just want to bring you up to date," he said. We settled at a table in the bar and he ordered a double martini for himself and a gin and tonic for me. I ordered spaghetti and meatballs, and he ordered a dozen oysters and a huge salad.

"Now isn't this pleasant?" My stomach roiled, and I doubted I could eat anything without puking. "You know, your buddy Agee is in the fold. And two others from Jesuit, who will remain unnamed. Now, I want you, kid." I knew that Phil had been called to Washington for interviews and a variety of tests, including a polygraph examination. But what did any of it have to do with me?

"Didn't your recent visit down south open your eyes to anything but feminine beauty?" If he mentioned the beautiful Alicia by name I would nail him. "Cuba may explode before we can finish our lunch. Is that what you want to see, a Communist nation ninety miles off our coast?"

"Castro's a Communist?"

"How can you breathe with your head buried in all that sand?"

"Look, even if I was interested, I've got to finish law school and two years of military service."

"Aren't you ever going to *listen* to me? We have ways of managing such things. All you have to do is come on board. But don't wait too long. Even a golden wonder like you can miss the boat."

I still didn't take my law studies too seriously, but I kept up with events in Cuba, having developed a recent special interest. I was alarmed and worried for Alicia and her parents by the increasing violence that was occurring now in Havana as well as throughout the countryside.

Ybor City was a hotbed of pro and con vocal support for the adversaries. Castro had spoken in Ybor City prior to all the commotion in the Sierra Madres, and to many Tampans, Fidel and his announced mission were worthy of support. Money was being raised all over the quarter for food and supplies.

I later discovered that Guy Bannister and David Ferrie ran a transit supply line through New Orleans. In fact, Ferrie was regularly in and out of Tampa and Miami, picking up money and supplies and flying them into the mountains of Cuba.

Meanwhile, shortly after my return from Cuba, the news was saturated with accounts of the 1956 Pulitzer Prize that had just been awarded to *Profiles in Courage.* The author was Congressman John F. Kennedy. The man never stops, I thought. And he had only recently survived a harrowing near-death surgical ordeal involving a lengthy coma. The public was furnished few details regarding this procedure. In fact, it would be many years before we learned just how much the Kennedy family had lied to us about Jack's health, lies that had enabled him to attain the presidency.

Allegedly, Kennedy's book was actually written by his congressional aide Ted Sorenson with Kennedy's guidance. But who can say for certain about such private endeavors? The book sold many thousands of copies thanks to the checkbook of Joseph P. Kennedy. Later that year, Congressman Kennedy almost garnered the vice presidential nomination — the publicity surrounding the Pulitzer Prize hadn't hurt — at the Democratic national convention in Chicago, barely losing to Adlai Stevenson. All of this was, in reality, the ground floor operation of Kennedy's impending presidential campaign of 1960.

The year 1957 brought considerable joy to the young congressman. After another miscarriage in 1956, Jackie Kennedy gave birth to a healthy daughter, Caroline, and for a time thereafter the grateful father scaled back on his adventures and devoted himself to the role of loving husband and happy family man. For a time.

The Author, Circa 1958

PART SEVEN

Days of Fatigues and Dress Blues

Ft. Bliss, El Paso, Texas, 1958

In the summer of 1958, I found myself on active military duty; an officer and a gentleman, as they say, by act of Congress. I could have deferred for a year to finish my last year of law school, but I wanted to get out of Tampa and save some money in the bargain.

I reported for basic training at the Military Police School at Fort Gordon, Georgia.

Shortly before I reported for Officer Basic Training, I met Pattie Ann Farrington, my future wife, at a small party given on Davis Island, one of my favorite hangouts since high school days.

My first post was in the city of El Paso across the Rio Grande from the Mexican border town of Ciudad Juarez and contiguous with the state of New Mexico further to the west. In 1958, El Paso was a city of fewer than 250,000 and rose almost 4,000 feet above sea level. Basic training back at Ft. Gordon had been a grueling romp in the park, while life in El Paso/Juarez would be high adventure. As a military police officer, I was assigned directly to the Provost Marshal's Office.

"You're young and inexperienced for such a command," said Colonel Gerald Momeyer, the crusty, no-nonsense Provost Marshal at our first meeting in his methodically organized office. "The position calls for the rank of major. Someone at the Pentagon must think highly of you. Well, we'll see when it comes time to file your first efficiency report."

He rose abruptly, stuck out his big hand and said: "Meanwhile, welcome aboard, Mettler. Do your job."

The job was to provide security for all classified projects being developed and implemented at Ft. Bliss, the U.S. Army's center for air defense and atomic weapons training, which included the White Sands Missile Firing Range. The area encompassed 104 square miles of west Texas and New Mexico desert land. Such duty required top secret security clearance for officers and men.

The Army Air Defense Center and School had only been established in 1957, so we were all breaking new ground. Ft. Bliss became the premier site for testing anti-aircraft equipment. Live

117

fire exercises at our McGregor Range in New Mexico featured the new Nike Ajax, Nike Hercules, Hawk and Sprint missiles in their developmental stage. The overall core mission was the development of doctrine and tactics, with an emphasis on training current and future soldiers to serve our country in time of need.

And Second Lieutenant George B. Mettler was responsible for the security arrangements pertaining to this entire operation! I was poleaxed by the assignment.

I tried to keep up with events in the "outside" world. President Eisenhower sent troops into Arkansas to enforce school integration, and Vice President Richard Nixon was booed and pelted with stones by Communist demonstrators in Lima, Peru during a tour of South America. In Rome, Pope John XXIII succeeded the deceased Pius XII, and the Brooklyn Dodgers moved to San Francisco. It seemed to me that little was sacred anymore.

At Ft. Bliss I was on duty twenty-four hours a day. I could never have survived had it not been for my efficient and loyal staff. At some top-secret areas within my overall responsibility, I was unaware of exactly what I and my men were protecting. But I had my instructions: Do my job. And my first major test wasn't long in coming.

One night I received a 2 a.m. phone call at my post BOQ from the duty officer at the MP station. No apologies for the early wakeup call; it was an emergency at the AWOC site — the top secret location of the Atomic Weapons Orientation Course. Students came from all branches of the government, military and civilian, and from allied countries around the world. There were colonels, generals, ambassadors and ministers of all ranks and nationalities among the ever-surging student body.

I was out of bed, armed and dressed in khaki uniform and physically on site in less than twenty minutes. A roving patrol car had picked me up at the BOQ and delivered me to the site. The sergeant of the guard was waiting for me at the front gate, the expression on his face alerting me to the level of pending concern.

The AWOC complex was one of the most security-conscious sites on Post; in the entire nation for that matter. I had no clear idea of what went on behind the gates and inside the imposing brick buildings. I knew only that there was a strict standing order regarding entering and exiting the position. You had a proper badge and identification card or you didn't enter. And when you left the site, you always departed empty-handed; no notes, sketches or photographs in your possession.

"What if the unauthorized person seeking entry outranks me?" I had asked Colonel Momeyer at one of our follow-up orientation meetings.

"On all such occasions, Lieutenant, no one outranks you. Not I, not the commanding general of the post, not even the President of the United States. Do I make myself clear?"

"Perfectly clear, sir." But I hoped in the worst kind of way that I would never have to clap President Eisenhower in chains.

"What's the trouble, Sergeant?" I asked the uptight sergeant of the guard who looked by now as if he was about to rectally deliver a full-term baby orangutan.

"We have an attempted unauthorized entry, sir." The fact that the sergeant was a twenty-year veteran of two wars was belied by the bloodless expression on his face. He escorted me to the guard shack just outside the main gate. Inside stood two of his armed troopers, both ashen-faced enlisted men, and two other men in civilian clothes.

"Are you the guy in charge of this here balls-up?" demanded a short bull of a man with angry eyes and a florid face that indicated too many drinks at the Officer's Club.

"Yes, sir. How can I help you, sir?"

"You c'n call off these snarlin' dogs an' get the hell out of our way. We got work t'do." He handed me an identification packet that I carefully studied and returned to him.

"I understand, General. I see that you are a registered student in the next AWOC Orientation Course. The course begins tomorrow — uh, later this morning, I should say — at 0800. Entry is not permitted prior to the designated date and time. You will be provided with proper credentials ..."

"You know where you can stick those credentials, Lieutenant. Do you know who I am? Do you know who my guest is? Are you too stupid ...?"

"Sir, please. I have my orders."

The other man stepped forward. "Listen to me, son. My name is ..."

"I know who you are, sir. I recognized your face immediately. But you simply are not authorized to enter the premises at this time. I will have to ask you both to leave."

"You what!" exclaimed the general. "An' what if I tell you we're goin' through that gate come hell or high water!"

"I would have to stop you, sir."

"You an' what army?" he demanded.

I looked meaningfully at my men, who stood their positions alertly, armed with side arms and carbines. I took a deep breath and said, "General, if you and the congressman won't leave quietly, I will have to take you both into custody."

His face reddened like an angry boil about to burst. "Wha's your name, boy. I'll have your ass boiled in oil for this."

I indicated the name tag above my breast pocket and said, "Do what you have to do, General. That's what I'm doing. Sergeant, place these men under arrest."

There was a uniform gasp in the little hut, and then the sergeant and his men stepped forward.

"Naw, cuffs won't be necessary," said the congressman in the distinctive drawl for which he was famously known. "We're leavin' now, Lieutenant. You done your job well." He turned to his stunned companion. "Wait for me in the car, Bert."

The starch in the congressman's voice seemed to penetrate the general's alcoholic haze. He visibly pulled himself together and started for the door, more stagger than swagger now. I said, greatly relieved, "Sergeant, have the General escorted to the car." Then to the congressman: "He can't be allowed to drive in his condition."

"No, son, I'll do the driving." He smiled and I could feel the strobe lights popping in his crowded hearing room back in D.C. "And I'll remember your name, too. You can make book on it." Then he took me by the arm and said, "Come, walk me out."

We went outside the hut and both of us paused to breathe in the fresh air wafting down across the mountains that ringed El Paso.

"The old boy's in a peck of trouble, no two ways about it," he said, lighting a cigarette. "I come out here on a little inspection tour, see, and I met up with ol' Bert at the Officer's Club. He was already in his cups, but the drinks kept comin' an' he just got worse and worse." He took a deep drag on his cigarette. "Man's a walkin' security risk, no two ways about it. You can rest assured he won't be attending the course that starts" — he looked at his watch — "soon."

We laughed and I followed him to the car, where he turned and stuck out his big hand and said, "You done good work, Lieutenant Mettler."

He got in the car, in the drivers' seat, and started the engine. The general was already asleep and snoring. The congressman chuckled and gave me a parting nod. I snapped a smart salute as the car pulled away and never once had the slightest idea that one day in the distant future I would work for one of the congressman's closest committee associates.

But that would come in another world in another time.

****

I spent two crowded years at Ft. Bliss, occasionally acting in concert with FBI and CIA agents in and around West Texas, New Mexico and Mexico proper. A couple of the agents worked openly with the Provost Marshal's Office and were fine fellows and well accepted by the officer corps. These aren't the guys I'm about to refer to now. *These* shadow figures came and went, and I don't think even the local agents were aware of their true identities or missions. These shadow figures thought that as CO of the Security Guard Detachment, I was in position to render assistance to both federal agencies.

Although I wasn't entirely convinced, I occasionally exchanged information with them and a few times delivered confidential information to a variety of safe-drop facilities. It was all a heady experience in the service of our country and world democracy. It was also beyond the scope of my duty assignment and possibly illegal.

They shouldn't have solicited such assistance, and *I* shouldn't have given it without permission. But I was coerced on grounds of critical government need. The conflict, they said, had been joined, and world survival was at stake. Sounded a lot like David Ferrie to me, but it was a pretty fair argument in view of recent world developments.

The Soviets had not only recently launched an intercontinental ballistic missile, they'd also put the first manmade satellite, Sputnik, into orbit, and it was as enormous a psychological coup as it was a scientific breakthrough. The world was mesmerized, and the line was relentless and unequivocal. Communists were intent upon colonizing the world, *they* said. America was at a crossroads in history, *they* said. Loyal citizens must let nothing stand in the way of the nation's defense, *they* said. It was my and every American citizen's duty to render aid. *They* said.

These were the voices of the shady, no-name characters that came and went under their own steam. Even Martin occasionally surfaced out of the mist swirling down off of the mountain tops.

Juarez, on the other side of the Rio Grande, was a cesspool of intrigue and corruption reflective of the national government in Mexico and, perhaps, of most governments everywhere. There were gangsters and spies, saints and sinners, con-men, whores, gamblers and dope dealers. It was an international city in those days. I'm not sure what we should call it in our present day: a cesspool of drug-infused crime and corruption? The mayor was said to be a contact CIA agent, as was his brother, the chief of police. They both worked harmoniously with the military police at Ft. Bliss. I was at a crossroad.

The upper-class establishments on the outskirts of the city hosted high-ranking military and civilian officials from the countries of the United Nations. The venues served the best food, the finest wines and liquors, and some of the loveliest companionship in the western hemisphere. Young girls, exquisite wild flowers from the fields and barrios of Mexico and beyond, were employed in the interest of enhanced international affairs.

Among the select guests, financial arrangements were explored, personal and state secrets exchanged, loyalties tested and diminished; in short, all the clandestine pursuits oxymoronically known within the discipline as "intelligence" operations. In due course, I became familiar with many of the waiters and working girls on that side of the river. All, of course, in the name of duty and personal honor.

On one of my solo-mission nights across the river I entered the men's room of one of the more popular glitter domes and immediately set to work. I located the waterproof packet submerged in the tank behind a designated commode. I removed the contents — a small leather pouch — inserted the envelope I'd been instructed to deliver, closed the packet and returned it to its place below the waterline. I washed and dried my hands, and, avoiding the urge to inspect my face in the mirror, I stepped into the ornate lobby. She was waiting for me.

"*Buenas noches, Jorge.*"

Her sudden approach startled me, but I quickly regained my composure as Rosaria Montez drew within perfume-smelling range. She was one of my favorites, a teenager from Taxco, who, along with her mother Juanita, served as go-betweens for the Nameless Ones. I never learned exactly how the ladies fit into the overall scheme of things, but ostensibly Juanita worked on the housekeeping staff while Rosaria, who was very popular with the incessant flow of highly-ranked visitors, served the cause of democracy in her own special way.

As usual, she looked gorgeous in a pale blue cocktail dress that plunged between her youthful breasts almost as far as her navel. With her sleek black hair pulled back and rolled on top of her head, she gave the stunning appearance of an Aztec sacrificial lamb. Which, I suppose, is what she was. "I saw joo enter *el bano* and waited to tell joo that I can stop work early tonight, eef joo can stay."

Her mispronunciation of English was almost cartoonish, and I loved it. "I'd like to, Rosaria, but tonight it's all business."

"Eef there ees to be entertainment afterwards, joo can ask for me."

"You know I don't like to see you here."

Her face dropped and she said in a whisper, "Joo know with joo eet ees different."

"I understand, but I can't help myself. It's the way I am."

"I like joo the way joo are." She actually blushed.

I smiled and touched her cheek lightly. *"Buenas noches, Rosaria. Vaya con Dios, y buenas suerte."*

My work for the evening was not finished; I had a responsive delivery to make back on the other side of the river. Meanwhile, I had a drink in the bar while I awaited the all-clear signal. It wasn't a long wait. A beautiful girl of fourteen or so, wearing a white organdy ball gown with a red carnation tucked behind her left ear — the sign that the exchange from behind the commode had been completed — approached me and asked in broken English if I would like a companion for the night.

"Sorry," I said, rising off my stool, "but I'm just on my way out."

"I say," came a phony British accent from a man in a tailored Saville Row suit leaning against the bar, "I wonder if I might stand in for Mr. America."

The girl laughed as if she'd understood what he meant and accepted his arm. He smashed out a foul-smelling foreign cigarette in an onyx holder, looked down his nose at me through horn-rimmed glasses as if he'd just robbed me of a precious jewel, and led his glittering trinket to the nearby dance floor.

I should have stayed with Rosaria.

They jumped me before I reached the International Bridge while I was still on the Mexican side of the river.

A man shoved into me on the sidewalk, knocking me into a narrow passage between two adjacent buildings. An accomplice waited in the alley, and I barely avoided having my skull crushed by a lead-weighted wooden club. I'd managed, however, to duck away from the blow and then rabbit-punched him in the sternum, spun on the balls of my feet the way I'd learned at OBT and smashed the first man's Adams's apple with the edge of my hand when he came rushing in from the sidewalk.

I had to move fast. Others might come at me in a second wave. Thankfully, the sidewalks were teeming with pedestrians, and some of them spotted the commotion in the alley. A woman screamed, a man shouted in a language I didn't recognize, and somewhere in the distance a police whistle sounded against the gusting breeze. I got the hell out of there as fast as I could.

There was no trouble at the gate; all the guards knew me on sight, and they passed me through without a document check. I returned to the post without delay and placed the pouch at the designated drop site — a hollowed-out bench leg in a garden spot near the post exchange. According to plan, it would be picked up within the hour.

I went straight to the BOQ, slamming and bolting the door behind me. My heart hammered, and my hands shook as I poured a shot of tequila and downed it straight. I gasped and poured a refill. For hours, I sat in the darkness beside the window that overlooked the parade ground. There would be no lights in the suite this night; I didn't want to make more of a target than I'd already been. Who were those guys? What was in that packet? Or had the attack not had anything to do with any of that smoke-and-mirror rigmarole? Would I ever know? Who would tell me? Who would I ask? Should I go to Colonel Momeyer and lay my head on the chopping block?

I felt a sickening chill throughout my body as I replayed the events in that alley and heard the ominous whistle of the club as it passed beside my ear. That bastard would have split my head wide open. And for what? What the hell was going on? I felt the blind fury boiling in my blood. What the fuck was the matter with *me?* What was *I* doing? I hadn't signed up for anything like this; who would be so stupid? Government service, my ass. If this was what government service was all about — what if they'd *killed* me; what if I'd killed one or both of them? None of it made sense.

Had I just learned the most fundamental lesson in life as well as government service? That none of it, nothing, ever had to make sense.

Jesus, I thought, what was I becoming? What had I become?

Admittedly, it was a time of surging national turbulence. The country was in the throes of its internal war over the issue of integration. The war was waged on an international stage via the technological innovation of television. A season of murderous rage was loose in the land. America the beautiful, the melting pot, the lady with open arms for all.

The government was a burning cauldron. And President Eisenhower was of little help, possessing little or no understanding of blacks and their aspirations. He later complained publicly that his appointment of Earl Warren as Chief Justice of the U.S. Supreme Court was the worst mistake he ever made as president. And it may well have been, but not because of the court's ruling in Brown vs. Board of Education, but rather for his complicity in the criminal cover-up of the facts concerning the assassination of President Kennedy.

Nevertheless, racial turmoil coupled with the prospect of nuclear annihilation was more than enough to unbalance even a nation as great as the United States. The dominant emotions of the time seemed to be fear, ill-directed hatred, and uncertainty.

Meanwhile, President Eisenhower sent U.S. Marines into Lebanon to resist a surge of Muslim rebels, Britain committed troops to support Jordan's King Hussein, and Communist forces shelled Nationalist Formosa. The world structure was unraveling before our eyes.

Earl Warren

The incident in Juarez focused my concern. Why wouldn't all of these faceless, nameless, spectral diabolists come out of the shadows and deal with me in the cold light of day? Who was the bogus British fop who had suddenly appeared on my action screen? Was *he* the boss running the whole show? Did anyone know the answer? Did anyone know *anything?* Jesus, I thought, if this was the way our government operated, what hope was there for the Republic? College-day echoes of the likes of David Ferrie, Clay Shaw and Guy Banister rattled around in my brain. Were they and their kind actually in charge? If so, then God help us all.

One day shortly after the Juarez episode, one of my more loose-lipped CIA contacts — at least he *claimed* to be CIA; how could you ever know for certain? — revealed to me on condition of utmost confidentiality that a new super-secret Company initiative was under way, one that was expected to pay spectacular dividends against our Soviet foes. "I can't tell you a lot about the operation, but I can assure you that your services will be much needed and appreciated. So be ready when they come calling."

Soon a pair of the most sinister operatives that had yet crossed my path slithered out of the shadows. From colleagues who had experience with them, I learned that they were former members of the Nazi Gehlen intelligence service from World War II. After the war, in response to the aggression of the Soviet Union, our government assimilated members of Hitler's intelligence agency into our Cold War apparatus. These ghouls were protected from war crimes investigations, resettled with new identities and made full-fledged partners in the defense of democracy.

This pair of operators, "Frick" and "Frack," I always called them, were the most amoral individuals I'd ever known. It's what we had become in our terror of Communism. Or was this what we had always been?

After a lot of digging and scraping, I learned that it was a mind-control / behavior modification research project designed to determine how ordinary people would react to interrogation and torture while under the influence of certain chemical stimulants. No one knew the formal name of the program, or if they did the name was never used in my presence. It would be a few years later — I was then a field agent with the FBI — before I learned that the official name of the program was MK-ULTRA.

The program was not new, it had originated in 1945 at war's end with something called Operation Paperclip, a program designed to recruit former Nazi scientists into our camp. These fiends were experts in torture, brainwashing, mind control and behavior modification. They were also war criminals, and some had already been prosecuted and convicted at the Nuremburg Trials. We stepped in with something called the Joint Intelligence Objectives Agency, and the ghouls began to work for us rather than face death.

They plied their trade under cover of Old Glory in such allied projects as ARTICHOKE and CHATTER, until in the early 1950s, CIA director Allen Dulles of later Bay of Pigs and Warren Commission infamy brought them into the MK-ULTRA compound and unleashed unholy hell on all perceived enemies. And although I didn't fully understand how the program was meant to work, I was soon enlightened about its more sinister implications.

One of my more cautious informants was a career officer with airborne/ranger qualifications and a healthy appreciation for all sorts of derring-do. He was an odd duck but a first-rate officer, competent in every way, and somehow he'd gained a modicum of information about this dubious operation. I never asked him how it was obtained, and he never explained.

"No, I don't know what it's called," he told me one day. "I'm told they get detached NATO participants out of the AWOC School all hot to party across the river in those health spas where they get 'em thoroughly primed and ready for testing. Then, unbeknownst to them, their food and drink is laced with a variety of chemicals such as scopolamine and the new super-secret LSD …"

"What the hell is that?"

"You'll find out. Just don't let yourself or any of your men …"

"Whoa! Me and my …"

"Let me finish." He was wound tight and cut me off. "After their guinea pigs have been sufficiently dosed, their behavior with the girls on duty is monitored with two-way mirrors, listening devices, and specialized photographic equipment. Secrets are blurted out, occasionally official documents are waved about, all in an effort to show the impressionable girls what big men they are playing their kinky games with."

My pulse raced as I thought of sweet Rosaria. Did she and her mother have any idea how they were being used? And the potential danger they were in?

"What the hell are we coming to? Nazi tactics and brown-shirt operators, for Christ's sake."

He shrugged. "But it's not for the likes of us to decide, is it? We get our orders and then do what we are told. It's the American way."

I was sickened by the whole mess. Not that I fully understood any of it. I didn't really know anything at that time. Still, I learned things from others — that high-ranking officers and diplomats were not excluded as test subjects, for one thing — but when I was pressured to provide a number of soldiers from my command for the purpose, I drew a line in the desert sand. Frick and Frack, however, were difficult men to refuse.

"We are not asking, Lieutenant. We are telling you what is to be done," Frick told me one day in a Teutonic fury. Or was it Frack?

"You have no choice but to follow orders," Frack said.

It was heated for a while, and it was only after I said that I would submit their request in writing to Colonel Momeyer, the Provost Marshal, that their own boss — whoever *that* was — called off the German wolf hounds. They were reassigned, I never saw or heard from them again, and I am eternally grateful.

Back in that early day, I did not know enough to understand just how complicated and corrupt things really were. How many Americans, for example, had any idea that the ridiculed abstract art movement in America of that day was funded and promoted by the CIA as a Cold War propaganda tool to use against the Soviet Union? Even the artists didn't know how and why they were being used or by whom.

Certainly I wouldn't have believed the number of movies that were sponsored in this cause, or the books that were published by CIA infiltrated and/or controlled publishing houses, or the number of magazines serving as Company fronts. No, unbeknownst to me, I was a pawn in a massive covert game of propaganda and subterfuge.

The Company line was compelling in the late fifties. The Soviet Union was determined to communize the world; America's survival was very likely at stake. Most Americans believed this back then, and I thought I believed it.

In Cuba, Batista was under attack, and Communists were questing for power less than ninety miles from the lovely Florida coastline. Atom bombs were being tested in the American desert — my command and others like it were largely responsible for the security of such operations — and school children were practicing their attack drills by learning to hide beneath their desks should such a cataclysmic blast suddenly engulf their world.

I crossed the river one night on a mission to make contact with Rosaria. I had to get her and her mother out of all of that dangerous mess. But she was nowhere to be found. She and her mother had simply disappeared. No one knew where they had gone; no one had ever heard of them. Had they simply been reassigned? I would never know.

As I crossed the ornately paneled lobby, a hand lightly touched my shoulder. "I say, Lieutenant, do have a drink with me in yonder bar."

It was the fop with the horn-rims, slicked-back hair, onyx cigarette holder and three-piece Saville Row suit, the character on the barstool the night I'd almost had my head split open. He said his name was Adrian St. Cloud, almost certainly a code name. It was infuriating and degrading to think I'd let myself get mixed up in anything with characters like Frick and Frack and this smarmy fop. Was he CIA or British intelligence? I interacted with him often in the years to come but never received an answer to my question.

"There is much I can't tell you, of course," he purred over a second glass of port while I nursed my only gin and tonic of the night. "And I am certain you appreciate the need for circumspection in such matters. These are precarious times, George — if I may be so informal — and we must be ever vigilant."

Although my distrust and dislike for the man remained undiminished, I was soon mesmerized by his pitch. It was like smoozing nose-to-nose with Rex Harrison, David Niven or Sir Laurence Olivier. That profound changes were about to occur on the world stage, there was no doubt. And certainly, as he knew I agreed, Communism should not be allowed to take hold and flourish in Cuba. Even should Batista have to go, St. Cloud said, an equally benign puppet would have to be installed in his stead.

"Cuba must continue to serve as a bastion against Communism on our national doorstep."

Was that a slip? Was he American after all? He put back his oily head and blew the foul-smelling smoke of his foreign cigarette above the table and hooted, "Oh this chap Castro will be allowed to preen and posture for the cameras — he was recently raising money again down in your Ybor City — but when the smoke clears he will have to hove to or else. And should he cause serious trouble for us, d'you see, well, plans for his 'removal' are already under way."

He read my expression and said, "Oh yes, you shouldn't be surprised. We always plan well in advance for all contingencies. Fidel's removal from the scene has already been scripted, under the guidance of Vice President Nixon in his role as White House Action Officer on the developing Cuba project."

I had no idea what he was talking about. *What* developing Cuba project? Were these guys always so loose lipped? And in any case, how could any of this murky high-level international intrigue possibly concern one of my inconspicuous rank? The answer soon became apparent enough.

"No!" I said adamantly, two nights later. My initial reaction to his scrubby request was an outright refusal. "I can't do that. I *won't* do it."

St. Cloud snapped his polished fingers toward our waiter and purred, "I say, I fancy it's time for another round, what?"

Tonight he was drinking double scotch like it was water. Did they all booze like this guy, I wondered, and like Martin? How did they get anything accomplished?

And then he suddenly plunged through the continuing smokescreen and nailed me between the eyes: "President Eisenhower, dear boy, wants you ..."

I'd said no, but I ultimately wore down under his persistent barrage and gave in to his request that I arrange an introduction to certain contacts from my youth. Contacts, he said, who were reputed to be very close to other significantly placed individuals on both sides of the present issues involving Cuba.

"Mind you, an introduction is all we are asking. You will be personally involved in no other way; I shall make all the necessary arrangements. We'll meet in Mexico City, d'you see. absolute cover and security assured. Full force and effect of U.S. government sanction."

And then a few nights later, I was more than a little surprised by Phil Agee's sudden appearance on scene. We met in an undistinguished Mexican restaurant rarely frequented by Americans. The site had been recommended to Phil prior to his arrival. By Adrian St. Cloud? We wore civvies, ties and sport coats, and Phil sported a military brush cut every bit as spiffy as my own.

"You're mighty wet behind the ears, Lieutenant, to be a commanding officer."

"Well," I replied, "as I was telling Ike the other night at supper ..."

We laughed and waited for the waiter to take our orders before indulging in biographical catch-up. In moments, the waiter returned with a bottle of red wine and a platter of spicy snacks. I had a momentary hesitation about eating or drinking anything on this side of the river. What might be in the food or drink? LSD? Scopolamine? More than likely my only contagion was self-induced paranoia-rampant. Although we were the only foreigners in the café, no one seemed to pay us any attention. But was that a sign of complicity in itself? There was a connecting bar on the other side of a beaded curtain, and we could hear live cantina music from inside.

I cut to the chase. "Why did Adrian want you to come here — just to see me?"

He was caught momentarily off guard and then said, "Who's Adrian?"

I laughed. "Tell me something, ol' buddy. Was that recruiter you told me about — the one back at Notre Dame — if it wasn't our old friend Martin, was he a tall cavernous fellow with a phony British accent who wore horn-rimmed glasses and smoked foul-smelling foreign cigarettes in an onyx holder?"

"Ain't he the damndest piece of work?" Phil laughed, too. "Now you know I've got to watch what I say, can't use names, can't refer by name to the agency I work for —"

"I thought you worked for the United States Air Force, Lieutenant."

"That's my cover, just like the Army is probably yours."

"Is that really what you think? Did Adrian tell you that?"

"Who's Adrian?"

"And the music goes round and round," I said.

We had a fine old time and after supper went into the cantina and had an even better time. I scarcely gave a thought to the possibility of two-way mirrors.

We said good-bye at the International Bridge on the Texas side of the river. Phil said, "Let's try to keep in touch. And best of luck to you in whatever you do."

"Same to you, buddy. I've got an idea we're both gonna need it."

It was one of the most prescient thoughts I would ever have.

The weekend meeting took place in a posh hacienda outside of Mexico City. This was shortly after J. Edgar Hoover had been forced to publicly acknowledge that there was indeed a loose-knit organization of mobsters operating inside the country. Operating, I thought, with government spooks and deviants.

Hoover had no alternative but to grudgingly come clean with the American public following the shocking incident that had taken place recently in Apalachin, New York. And although no convictions resulted from the arrests, dozens of important people were identified, many of whom had been previously unknown to police and public.

The main engagements of the war against the Mafia would have to wait for another presidential administration to build a fire under the foot-dragging FBI director. And I had no idea that I would have a hand in setting that fire.

In the meantime, I found the Mexico City meeting instructive. Although Adrian St. Cloud had been true to his word and I was in no way involved in any of the sessions, I kept my eyes and ears wide open. Over the lavish food and wine and palatial comforts of my remote sitting room, I monitored the incessant comings and goings of the night. And what I earned for my attention was more important than a Ph.D. diploma.

I knew that back in November of 1956, Fidel Castro's "invasion" of Cuba had launched from Mexico on a boat named Granma that transported eighty-two men, weapons and ammunition. The landing had been a fiasco, and only Castro and twelve survivors had escaped to their mountain sanctuary. On Christmas day of that year, Castro — a Christ figure in fatigues and combat boots — had announced to Batista and the world that: "Now we are going to win!"

Now Castro was preparing to move against the Batista government in Cuba and was here in Mexico City again to organize the effort. Citizens and aliens alike were abandoning the island nation in droves in fear for their lives. I thought with a heavy heart of my many friends and acquaintances and their families. I especially thought sadly of Alicia Valez.

Fulgencio Batista

And because it was possible that Castro's rag-tag revolutionary mob might carry the day, bets had to be hedged. That's why tonight the hacienda was crowded with so many people I didn't know: Adrian's colleagues from Washington, Santo's people from Florida, Marcello's New Orleans workers, and a swarm of Cubans of varying ages and temperaments. Would Castro himself make an appearance?

I wouldn't have been as shocked by government collusion with the mob had I been aware of the precedent set back in 1942 during WWII and the deal struck between the U.S. Navy and Lucky Luciano for dock security.

Of course, I was unclear as to exactly what it was that St. Cloud wanted Santo's people to do on behalf of the government's interests in the volatile Cuban situation. If the CIA was about to enlist Mafia assistance in support of Batista as a hedge against encroaching Communism in the hemisphere, then Fidel Castro's days in the sun could be counted on one hand.

But this was mere supposition on my part. At that time I knew nothing more about the situation than what I have reported. I'd been asked to serve as an intermediary in setting up the meeting and making the introductions, and Adrian St. Cloud's people would handle things from that point on. I realize today that my assistance had been unnecessary. It was St. Cloud's way of keeping me on the leash.

Everything went as planned. Two or three phone calls, starting with Nick Carlotta, had set the venture in motion. I think Frank Ragano was chosen as the point man, but I never saw him or Santo, and I was gone by the time of their arrival, if they ever showed.

Two years later I learned that the actual purpose of the Mexico City meeting was to funnel CIA money through the mob in *support* of Castro and his revolutionary efforts against Batista, just in case. By that time, however, I thought that nothing had the capacity to shock me anymore.

I had much to learn.

****

"I now pronounce you man and wife."

Pattie and I got married in Tampa and honeymooned in New Orleans. It was not a rousing success. And looking back, I knew even then that Pattie had dreams of her own, and I'm sorry I was unwilling and unable to help her achieve them. I take full blame for our breakup some ten years later, but of course I'd had no idea that I would meet Darlene and my life would change forever.

When Pattie and I returned to El Paso from our honeymoon in the French Quarter, we took a small apartment a short distance off Post. We would not be long in residence. I had decided against an Army career and planned to complete my final year of law school in Florida.

We settled into the Aquilla house. Mama and John were in Georgia. I started school early in September, the campaign for the presidency was nearing the finish line. I contributed small amounts of our savings, placed placards on the car, handed out literature, and spoke up on every occasion that came my way. John Kennedy was my candidate. Anyone but the thuggish Richard Nixon. Pattie, too, was for Kennedy, while most of our friends supported Nixon.

I've often wondered what the outcome might have been had the public at large known the extent of JFK's philandering ways and his precarious medical condition. He had women coming and going like running water: secretaries, movie stars, randy housewives, adventurous college girls. His health was a truly serious matter. Already he had been given the last rites of the Catholic Church following surgeries that left him near death for months at a time.

In 1947, Jack was first diagnosed with fatal Addison's disease. It was thought that he wouldn't live out the year. He survived but could never be cured. Doctors knew, however, and Jack knew that he was destined to die young. The diagnosis explained so many nuances of his many recurrent illnesses. It also explained his deeply fatalistic attitude toward life. He determined to live every minute as though it might be his last.

But at the time the public had no awareness of any of this. There was no Internet, no system of blogging to reach the masses. For the first time, television was a major factor in the outcome of an election. Kennedy was mobbed in the streets, especially by female supporters of all ages. Nixon, well, I think the four face-to-face televised debates made all the difference. Viewers saw the candidates standing a couple of feet apart, and it was like posing actors William Holden alongside an unshaven Ernest Borgnine. Sorry, Ernie.

Nevertheless, it was the closest election in U.S. history. And there were rumors and accusations that Kennedy's father had bought the election and that old Joe's mobster cronies had falsified the vote in many jurisdictions, especially in mob-controlled Chicago. It would be some time before I learned that the claims were not merely sour grapes by the losers. I also learned, however, that playing it safe, the mob had contributed just as much to Nixon, who had been in their pocket almost from his entry into politics.

Kennedy was declared the winner, and I couldn't have been happier. How could I, or anyone, have imagined the heartbreak that his victory would lead us, our country and the world to?

****

I remember a conversation I had with an old friend in the waning days of the presidential election.

"There will be a blood bath someday soon, mark my words." Andy Melendez was a second generation American, and we'd grown up together on the playground and later at Jesuit High School. I knew how serious-minded he was. A recent mayoral campaign in Tampa had illuminated the entrenched racial prejudice that still infected the local conscience. The Sicilian-Italian candidate was pilloried by the establishment opposition as a mere stooge of the underworld, a pilot fish for a Mafia takeover of the city. The charges drew widespread attention and once again Tampa was unfavorably portrayed in the national media as a "mobster-controlled hell-hole." Italian, Sicilian, Spanish, Cuban, it was all the same: foreign blood, foreign morals and beliefs.

I soon learned that many of our friends and acquaintances were involved in one way or another as government agents, Castro loyalists, and/or exile freedom fighters with the increasing turmoil in the Caribbean. Schemers on both sides of the fence seemed to have little or no concern regarding the security of their feelings and intentions. Emotions were running so high that threats and fist fights were every-day occurrences, often between old friends and even feuding family factions.

After the success of the revolution, citizens and aliens alike had fled Cuba in droves. I'd tried in every way I knew to locate Alicia Velez and her parents, without success. The whole family had disappeared. And although Batista had been deposed, he'd escaped with his life and was living in grand exile with his stolen millions in Paris. The funds and properties of American individuals and corporations doing business on the island had been confiscated by the revolutionary government in the name of *socialismo*. Meyer

Lansky and the other Mafia kingpins had left Havana after the takeover, forfeiting their property and business interests, legal and illegal.

Santo, however, had stubbornly remained behind, unwilling to run. Nevertheless, most of the hotels and casinos had been destroyed by Castro's revolutionary mobs, and the few that remained in operation with government approval had no business to attend to. There were no tourists, no high-rollers. The owners were forced by Castro's government to pay their employees to stand around and look at each other. I found it difficult to believe that no one in positions of importance could have seen it coming.

That night when the *Fidelistas* entered Havana — New Year's Eve, 1959 — the streets were suddenly choked with swarms of ecstatic revelers, delirious in their joy in being rid of the brutal Batista, oblivious to the imminent terror about to befall them in the coming hours, weeks, months, and decades that lay ahead. But shouldn't *someone* have known? The *Batistianos,* the Fat Cats of corporate America, the mob, the CIA? Were they all nothing more than a cluster of ostriches with their heads stuck in the crystal sands? Or was something else at play? Time would answer that question clearly enough for those willing to see the truth.

Within weeks of Castro's victory, Santo had been arrested and sentenced to death by firing squad. Had he completely misjudged the tenor of the revolution by not fleeing at once? Or was another tune being played for the international audience? After some months in jail, Santo was released by way of a "private arrangement" between one of his lawyers, Frank Ragano, and Castro's brother, Raul. Santo was soon back in Florida at the head of his intact family claiming to have lost more than 20 million dollars in the Cuban debacle.

But he was alive and healthy, and soon the U.S. government would seek his aid in its clandestine efforts to assassinate Fidel Castro.

Although I tried to concentrate on my legal studies, I discovered that I wasn't off the Company hook just yet. Martin and Adrian St. Cloud both popped up at irregular intervals, always singing the same tune. So far, I'd remained stubbornly unwilling to dance. St. Cloud seemed to have taken the lead, but maybe Martin was just strutting along to a different rhythm.

St. Cloud had learned that during my first year in law school in Macon, Georgia, I had been acquainted with the son of the president of the provisional Cuban government proclaimed by Castro immediately after the success of the revolution prior to his publicly going Communist. I'd tried unsuccessfully to arrange a meeting between the two but in fact had lost all contact with my schoolmate. Meanwhile, I'd learned through Tampa sources that Phil Agee had been posted by the CIA to his first duty assignment in Bogotá, Columbia, under the comic-opera pseudonym of Jeremiah Bopp! I'd also learned that a number of other former unnamed Jesuit colleagues had jumped aboard the Agency train.

Around this time, I became personally aware of David Ferrie's quixotic air-support activities for and against Castro. It was impossible ever to know for certain which side of the coin the buffoonish figure from New Orleans was polishing. I didn't see him while he was in Tampa, apparently he had deteriorated dramatically since I'd known him in New Orleans.

Eastern Airlines had fired him for a string of homosexual escapades with young boys. He'd continued working in New Orleans in a murky arrangement with Clay Shaw, Guy Banister and Carlos Marcello, his employment based on his outstanding ability to fly any make of aircraft under all conditions. Now, he'd flown his two-engine Cessna into one of Tampa's private airports and was said to have unloaded enough weapons and ammunition to supply a combat battalion. He then took off for parts and reasons unknown deep in the Florida Keys.

I also had brief contact with still another character with whom I'd crossed paths back in New Orleans. Namely one Jack Ruby, then of Dallas, Texas.

Easily recognizable, he was dressed exactly the same as he'd been on other occasions when I'd encountered him. Dark tailored suit in spite of the tropic heat, dark hat with the brim pulled down over his left eye, starched white shirt and a black silk tie. He was eating lunch with some men from the exile community when I entered the restaurant on Dale Mabry Avenue, and a couple of his companions exchanged greetings with me. Tampa was that kind of community back in that day. Ruby merely nodded, and I didn't stop to speak to him.

Exactly what he was up to and on whose behalf he was working, I could never clearly establish. According to Andy Melendez, Ruby had come to Florida for an unsuccessful exile supply operation. Something to do with a failed attempt to purchase vehicles for the ubiquitous exile conspirators in and around Key West, the Everglades, New Orleans, Mexico and Guatemala.

Jack Ruby

"Of course it failed," Andy laughed one morning over coffee and pancakes in the law-school cafeteria. "According to Santo, everything that *cabron* touches goes down the drain. It's probably why Capone chased him out of Chicago so many years ago, banishing him down to New Orleans and Dallas."

"What about his drug business? Has that gone down the drain too? I always heard that he ran drugs in Tampa out of Drew Field back during the war."

"I don't know nothin' about drugs, and don't want to know."

* * * * * * * * * * * * * *

My classmates were more enervated by the turbulent drama in the Caribbean than by their grueling legal studies. Everyone knew what was going on.

Throughout the spring we listened to short-wave radio reports on our transistors morning, noon and night. Even a date for the Grand Invasion was openly discussed around the campus, in Tampa, and particularly in the enclaves of Ybor City. How incompetent could the CIA be? And how involved was the new president?

Andy Melendez was a fount of information. I soon learned that the primary training base for the invasion team, a relatively small band of men known as Brigade 2506, was in the jungles of Guatemala. Was Jeremiah Bopp, aka Phil Agee, in any way involved? The mission had been designed and approved by members of the Eisenhower administration prior to the 1960 election of John Kennedy.

Many of my friends and acquaintances and their relatives were committed participants who had been on board since before Kennedy assumed the presidency. The name or party affiliation of the man in the oval office made no difference. All that mattered was the mission objective: the overthrow and death of Fidel Castro.

But to compound the dangers involved, more than a few of my friends and their relatives were Castro agents working under deep cover. They knew all about the impending invasion. Were all of our leaders asleep at the switch? What were Martin and St. Cloud doing? Was so much apparent hands-off stand-and-watch conduct evidence of incompetence or connivance? The atmosphere was hallucinogenic.

The invasion at the Bay of Pigs on April 17, 1961, as the world knows, was an unmitigated disaster. Poorly conceived and planned, it had no hope of success. It was so badly handled that a detached observer must wonder, even in this day, whether or not its defects were created by design and, if so, then by whom and why?

Castro had clearly been forewarned, and the public opinion about the causes of the failure was that there was no hope of success without massive U.S. airpower support, support that President Kennedy allegedly disallowed at the last moment. The brigade was decimated on the beach.

This explanation was drummed into the American people by an unrelenting news media and promoted by military and civilians from all corners of our society. Our new president, in office barely three months, publicly took full responsibility for the failure.

I would later learn that President Kennedy had *approved* the final use of air cover with covert non-U.S. bombers before he went to bed the night prior to the invasion. It was, in fact, canceled the next morning by Special Assistant to the President McGeorge Bundy. The president publicly took the blame, yes, but privately he railed at the CIA for misleading him and vowed to dismantle the Agency altogether upon his reelection. I also learned that CIA director Allen Dulles had chosen to vacation in Puerto Rico on the morning of the invasion, thereby leaving all command decisions to secondary leaders with little or no combat or command experience!

And the most important information concerning the failed invasion involved the controlling influence of the super-secret National Security Council Directive 5412.

The public remained unaware of former Vice President Nixon's hands-on role in the development of the initial invasion plan and the concurrent CIA operations to assassinate Fidel Castro with the help of Tricky-Dick's long-time Mafia associates. Indeed, his fear exposing his illicit participation in the botched scheme to overwhelm Cuba was at the core of then President Nixon's Watergate debacle.

But at the time, the exile community and a preponderance of the American people blamed Kennedy alone for the failure of the invasion. Many of my friends and their relatives were devastated by the tragedy, and more than a few of them openly vowed vengeance even if it took the rest of their lives to achieve. Certainly the Trafficante family was opposed to Kennedy. They detested both Jack and Robert, especially the latter, as a result of their unpleasant experiences with the brothers in the various congressional investigations of recent years. And with Jack's appointment of Robert as Attorney General, Santo and his people could foresee nothing but trouble ahead.

But JFK's call to government service stirred me: "Ask not what your country can do for you. Ask what you can do for your country." I was still an ambitious young man and determined to accomplish something of merit with my life. I just didn't know for certain exactly what direction my efforts should take.

A few weeks before graduation, one of Santo's closest associates invited me to lunch at one of Don Santo's favorite Ybor City restaurants. Santo was in Miami on business, my host said as we settled into chairs at Santo's table in the Columbia Restaurant, at that time the flagship of all such eateries in Ybor City. And over a sumptuous meal of linguini and veal parmesan, I was extended an offer that I almost could not refuse.

"Friendship," said my host in a soft accented voice that carried great sincerity, "next to family, is the most important thing in a man's life. A man alone stands little chance of success in society. But a young man with good friends can enjoy an unlimited future." I could hear the echo of Mr. San Marco's admonitions in every word. "The law is a fine profession, advantageous in business as well as politics. Santo is well aware of your record. We are certain that, given your intelligence and ambition, you will make a fine lawyer."

I had known this man from my earliest days on the playground, and he had actually served my skittish mother as a helpful caretaker of her Sonny Boy. Was he now representing her or Santo? He went on to explain that even though as an Anglo I could never aspire to become one of Santo's primary lawyers — he was by this time represented by two of my long-time friends — as soon as I passed the bar and set up practice in Tampa, or Miami should I prefer, Santo would see to it that sufficient business would come my way to enable me to lead a good life.

"I don't know what to say. He seems to always be around when I need a helping hand." I really was perplexed by such a gratuitous and unsolicited intercession.

"That's what friends are for," my friend told me with a smile. "We have always known you would do well. Your dear mother will be so proud, as she always has been of your accomplishments."

I didn't know what to say, so I said nothing. He wasn't finished.

"Santo, all of us, were impressed by the way you managed matters in Mexico City. And now let us be candid. Your friendships in Tampa will prove most beneficial in the coming years. You will be on a first-name basis with police, bail bondsmen, judges, prosecutors, defense attorneys, politicians and prominent businessmen." He smiled.

"And with your many important women friends, I might add."

Even I laughed. I wondered if he was aware of my youthful relationship with my *goomada* those many years ago. But he said nothing more on this subject.

"Georgie, you have our utmost confidence, and you can be of considerable assistance to our interests and to those of our friends. But I need not tell you how much Santo wishes you to understand that in no way would you ever become involved in the "Family" business. You will serve only as an attorney, a well-connected Anglo attorney with impeccable credentials in the Anglo community. And never for one moment should you underestimate the power of public relations and public image."

I sat in silence for a long moment and then thanked him for his considerations and said how much I hoped he would pass my sincere appreciation on to Santo. Then I reached inside my jacket pocket, withdrew a folded cablegram and passed it to him. He opened it and read with a deep frown cutting into his swarthy face. Then he carefully refolded the cablegram and handed it back to me.

"Well, you have chosen an interesting way of life. Santo will be advised."

The cablegram read:

YOU ARE OFFERED APPOINTMENT SPECIAL AGENT GRADE GS10. REPORT NINE a.m. JUNE TWELFTH ROOM FIVE TWO THREE ONE JUSTICE BUILDING NINTH STREET AND PENNSYLVANIA AVENUE NORTHWEST WASHINGTON, D. C. NO PUBLICITY SHOULD BE GIVEN APPOINTMENT.   ADVISE   IMMEDIATELY   OF ACCEPTANCE. LETTER FOLLOWS.

It was signed: J. Edgar Hoover.

A young colonial patriot called to duty by George Washington could have experienced no greater elation; it was the proudest day in my life. Perhaps I should have heeded the Biblical admonition that pride goeth before a fall.

Fidel Castro

PART EIGHT

FBI in War and Peace

My government career got off to less than an auspicious start. On my first night in Washington, after a day spent sightseeing, I went to bed early in my hotel room intending to get a good night's sleep prior to reporting to FBI headquarters at the Justice Department the next morning. Unfortunately, a boisterous party at the end of the hall kept me awake.

Finally I went to the door and looked out and found the party door standing open. Men and women in varying stages of undress were milling about, and just imagine my shock upon seeing President Kennedy's brother-in-law, movie star Peter Lawford, with a glass of whiskey in hand, wearing a dress shirt, tie and a pair of boxer shorts.

I shut the door and wondered just what the hell I'd let myself in for. "Ask not what your country can do for you," I muttered, "ask what you can do for your country."

Entering the new agent's training class was like stepping through the looking glass. We played games directed by grown men, games that we had only dreamed of as boys. The sixteen-week training session that followed my appointment was a grueling experience, a blend of army boot camp and grad-school grind. Some class work was held in the Justice Department Building but most of our time was spent at the FBI Academy located nearby on the Quantico Marine Corps base in Virginia. A hundred or so recruits were drilled by experts in such matters as the U.S. Constitution, federal rules of criminal procedure, the Top Secret FBI Hand Book and the Manual of Rules and Regulations.

Experienced agents lectured on investigative techniques and arrest procedures, and laboratory experts dazzled us with the arcane mysteries of their specific specializations. There was no reference, however, to MK-ULTRA and mind control programs. But many hours were devoted to the menace of Communism and undercover defensive operations euphemistically referred to as tradecraft. Mr. Hoover and hence the agency he commanded was absolutely consumed with matters pertaining to the Communist Party and its avowed mission of world dominance through subversion, espionage and sabotage. There was no mention of organized crime or use of the word Mafia.

It was a relentless regimen day and night. Nor was all of our work confined to the classroom. We spent hours on the firing range by day, followed by numbing physical training activities in the gymnasium by night. We learned to function under pressure with our wits, brains, hands and feet, as well as with guns and a wide assortment of James Bond technical gadgetry. In short, we learned to defend our lives and to kill when necessary in the pursuit of self-defense, justice, and national security.

And underlying all the instruction was one basic and continuous message that came at us like a Hindu mantra: the FBI was the finest investigative agency in the history of the world; J. Edgar Hoover was the greatest administrator of all time; and the agent corps was the most elite group of men ever assembled. Men, mind you. There was no female influence in that day among the agent cadre. I wondered what we were supposed to do when a woman's investigative skill was required by circumstances of a particular case: wear a wig and falsies?

We were assured time and again that: "The FBI has never done anything that was not entirely in the public interest." And the one inviolable rule of the FBI force was: *Never to embarrass the Bureau.*

Although this is what I had wanted since childhood, by degrees I found myself troubled by certain aspects of what I was learning about the Bureau and Mr. Hoover. I couldn't help remembering the stories I'd heard from my high school friend Bill Ferlita at the FBI office back in New Orleans. But most of his revelations had been hearsay. My impressions, now based on what I was seeing and hearing, were beginning to seem incontrovertible.

The Bureau was populated by fine men, yes, but there was an incestuous elitism about the organization that was more than a little troubling. Moreover, there was an overt Kennedy bias against John and Robert, an exclusion of minorities — besides no women, there were no blacks and Hispanics, and no more Jews than you could count on one hand — and an obsession with image to the detriment of substantive performance.

To think, no blacks among the agent force. Like I had done concerning the absence of female agents, I tried to imagine the investigation of crime in locations such as Harlem by teams of clean-cut white men in tailored suits, snap-brim hats and shiny shoes. Meanwhile, black citizens by the thousands were being abused by white law enforcement officers all across the land with tear gas, night sticks, whips and guns for having the temerity to demand to share such privileges of citizenship as drinking fountains, rest rooms, restaurants, public conveyances and classrooms.

The seemingly perverse character and quixotic personality of J. Edgar Hoover distressed me. I wasn't even out of training school, and the idol of my youth was beginning to resemble a petty tyrant with feet of soiled clay.

I was pleased along with the rest of the country to applaud Commander Alan Shepard's sub-orbital flight, the first for America. But soon consternation would replace applause when East Germany constructed the Berlin Wall in a provocative gesture that might possibly lead to WWIII, and on the other side of the world South Africa left the British Commonwealth in an equally provocative gesture that might, well, who could say what might happen in that part of the world?

Midway through the training grind when we thought we couldn't take it much longer, we were given a weekend leave. I flew home and spent as much time with Pattie as I could. It was a useful break, but it was impossible to avoid all the matters that had begun to cause such bilious nights back at NAC. So soon after the debacle at the Bay of Pigs, I now learned that all covert operations in Cuba had continued with even more pressure to succeed. Bobby, it was said, was putting increased pressure on the CIA to assassinate Castro. Ybor City was a hive of activity pro and con.

"And you know all this for sure?" I asked one of my good friends after the failed invasion, a former FBI agent who had left the Bureau in disgust and was now practicing law in Florida.

"I was in Miami, meeting with colleagues at the JM/WAVE Station," he said as we entered the comfort of his cozy den in a fine neighborhood in Palma Ceia. His wife had served us mixed drinks and then gone out shopping. "The Kennedys had launched something called Operation Mongoose, with Bobby in charge. Its sole mission was to assassinate Fidel Castro."

"Jesus Christ!" I exclaimed.

"No, He had already opted out. It was Bobby and the drunken madman, Wild Bill Harvey, who were in charge of getting things done. Harvey is in charge of all agency JM/WAVE operations. He's a drunken lout, a former FBI man who had built a reputation as a daring and effective spymaster in Berlin after the war. He'd always hated the Kennedys and made no secret of his feelings. Then Bobby complicated matters by bringing in a man to directly supervise Mongoose, Edward Lansdale."

He gave me a trenchant look and I shook my head no. "A legendary counterinsurgency expert; army general in WWII, then OSS and finally CIA. Of course, the whole Castro thing was an operation doomed for disaster."

I was having a tough time getting my arms around all of this, and my friend saw it.

He gave me another stiff drink and said, "Okay, now swallow your drink and then see if you can swallow this. When it became obvious that Mongoose wasn't taking off, another former G-man was enlisted to bring in some help from some of his friends, the ones with the funny names. After leaving the Bureau, Robert Maheu had become a shady private eye with a unique clientele. He orchestrated the bugging of the Las Vegas hotel room of TV comedian Dan Rowan, who his client believed was sleeping with his client's mistress, singer Phyllis McGuire. His client was Momo Giancana, Mafia overlord of Chicago."

"Jesus Christ!" I said again.

"You keep calling on that guy. I tell you, He's not involved in this caper."

I finished my drink and stood up.

"Sit down and you'll hear the rest of the story." I sat and he said, "Maheu's client list included not only Giancana, but Johnny Roselli and your buddy Santo. Maheu has enlisted them along with Marcello in the plot to assassinate Castro. The deal has been struck, money's changed hands, and now they're all involved in Mongoose."

Through clenched teeth I asked, "And the Bureau?"

He scoffed at the notion. "A legion of blind mice from Edgar on down."

I slept that night in a boozy fog of fear and loathing.

"I can't believe they're so strict," Pattie said one night at one of her favorite restaurants.

I laughed at her innocence and said, "The official dress code of a G-man ought to be a strait jacket. It's nerve-wracking." I waved at old acquaintances as they passed our tables and smiled fondly at a few of the wives. Few had any idea of where and why I had been absent from the city for such a lengthy interval. "We don't know from one day to the next whether we'll make it another hour. We've lost a half dozen recruits already."

"Why? What did they do?" Pattie asked.

"Who knows, they don't give out reasons. In fact, the instructors don't even mention the sudden absences. One day a guy's here, the next day he's gone." I laughed again, but it wasn't a mirthful sound. "One guy got bounced because someone, probably Hoover, decided his ears were too big."

"Weren't his ears the same size when they offered him the appointment? Or did they grow while he was in training?"

We were laughing together, but neither of us thought it was funny. "The old man's hovering presence is truly ominous," I said. "And our biggest test is yet to come. In the last week of the training cycle each agent recruit has to enter the director's office and meet the Great One in person. Say hello, shake his hand, and try not to vomit on his desk or faint from nervous excitement."

Pattie was laughing in silent gasps now, holding her napkin to her lips. There was really nothing more to say. We danced for a while, strolled in the garden and went home. When we undressed for bed Pattie asked, "Is any of this allowed, or is dismissal hanging in the eaves?"

She was so blond and pretty, so warm and affectionate. What the hell was the matter with me? Why didn't I just mail in my resignation and set up housekeeping right here at home? And do what, I thought. Practice law; sell insurance or used cars? How long would it be before Agee, Martin, or Adrian St. Cloud would come calling?

But in the final days of the training cycle, I came upon the startling discovery that had the potential for destroying my Bureau career before it even got started. Only now was the subject of organized crime dealt with in anything more than superficial notice. One of our instructors was naming the *alleged* current leaders of the *alleged* Mafia — the organization that according to Hoover didn't really exist — identifying each individual by name and photograph. There were thought to be twenty-four criminal "families" ranged about the United States, he said, each with a leader known as a "don" or "godfather," and a support cadre of inferior officers called "capos," who in turn directed the ordinary "soldiers" under their command.

Many of the black and white photographic faces I knew. In New Orleans I'd seen Tony Accardo of Chicago and Frank Costello of New York many times, and of course Carlos Marcello of New Orleans and Dallas. But Carlos wasn't on their photographic screen. He and/or New Orleans were never even mentioned during the course of our instruction. Oversight due to bureaucratic incompetence or … . I wish I had an answer for you even at this late date.

But there *he* was: Santo Trafficante Jr., age 38, 6'1", 185 pounds, thick black hair and deep-set dark eyes. But they were wrong, the greatest law enforcement agency in the history of the world was flat-out wrong! Santo stood just under six feet and weighed about 165 pounds. His hair was thin and sandy-colored, and his eyes, behind horn-rimmed glasses, were a startling emerald green. But they had a name right out of my childhood. Should they learn about my relationship with Santo and his people, they would recall my credentials before I could begin to swear my loyalty to J. Edgar Hoover and the United States of America.

But they didn't know, or didn't care, and I figured that by the time they made the discovery or their attitude changed, I would be beyond their sphere of control. For you should remember that my fondest hope in life since childhood had been to be a writer. The FBI had finally become for me the best method that I could see to obtain the kind of factual information that would make my fiction sing.

But now I was beginning to wonder how much I would learn about all of this Mafia business from the instruction in NAC. No one seemed to know anything about the mob, little or nothing about wiseguy speech patterns and behavior. As we have previously seen, they didn't even know the true name of the organization. Remember, for decades Hoover had denied there was anything such as a Mafia. But now here they were, at least referring to the Mafia, without knowing the real name of the outfit.

I'm not even certain when and how *I* had first come to know that the members didn't refer to themselves as the Mafia. That was outsider terminology. Internally the organization was known as *Cosa Nostra*, Our Thing. And the few times that such an appellation was used here in training school the instructors misnamed it La *Cosa Nostra*, which translated as The *Cosa Nostra*, which in turn meant The Our Thing. The finest law enforcement agency in the history of the world?

The great day arrived at last. I walked across the wide pile carpet in the director's office on the sixth floor of the Justice Department, shook hands with the pudgy little man I had admired all of my life, listened to a few rote words of encouragement and then proceeded on my way as the next recruit entered the room on cue to perform his act of obeisance.

With badge and credentials in hand, George Barry Mettler was a bona-fide G-man. James Bond, Graham Greene and John LeCarre could seek other work; there wouldn't long be room in the field for all of us.

****

"It was incredible," said Fred Osborn one night in a Springfield coffee house. I'd filed my surveillance report and would be heading back down to Carbondale early the next morning. "Colleagues at SOG say you could hear him bellowing all through the halls of Justice. As soon as Jack named him Attorney General, Bobby went to work on his two primary goals of destroying organized crime from the top down and severing its corrupting influence with American labor unions."

"Bobby considered both unfinished business from his time as chief counsel to the McClellan Senate Crime Commission. He began an immediate overhaul of the organized crime unit set up by President Eisenhower after the Apalachin debacle. Ike's special prosecutors had accomplished absolutely nothing, and Bobby resolved to fix that post haste. He was like a bull in the proverbial china shop."

My head was reeling because Bobby now had a third major goal, that of assassinating Fidel Castro. Was Fred unaware of Operation Mongoose, or was he holding back for a reason? Was he not in the loop on the hook-up between Bobby and the mob in the government's plan to kill Castro? I decided to play my cards close to the vest.

"Bobby had already had a history of combative face-offs with Hoover and was aware of the Old Man's lackadaisical attitude toward so-called organized crime."

"No such thing as a Mafia," I scoffed.

"Yeah, but there were reasons for his attitude. One was his fear of corruption of the agent force. After all, as it was often said, cops and robbers are two sides of the same coin. And with the non-existent Mafia, it was a prime risk. All that money; the temptations were so great. Hoover knew very well how *he'd* been tempted and corrupted over the years and realized that he had to exercise extreme caution to insure the reputation of his agency and his reputation as the government's finest administrator of all time." He laughed. "After all, we had the Communist menace to command our attention, and there weren't many G-men likely to turn Bolshevik."

I laughed too and tried to interpose a few questions. "Are all of those stories about Hoover ..."

"Later, kid, you can't swallow everything at once. Now listen up. Even those in the FBI who knew there was an organized criminal conspiracy at work in this country knew little or nothing about the organization itself. We didn't know its real name, didn't know how it was organized, didn't know how it worked or who its leaders were. We had no mission to destroy this non-existent organization, and even if we wanted to get them, we hadn't a clue how to go about it. Nothing could be done without Hoover's okay, and that wasn't going to happen."

"Until Apalachin," I said.

"Bingo," Fred almost yelled, looked around the café and lowered his voice. "In 1957, organized crime became a public issue. Hoover *had* to get off the pot. And you know how clever he is. *He* took credit for everything that transpired thereafter. *He* discovered an organized criminal group at work in the United States. So he created the Top Hoodlum Program and set out to go after the mob with the same tactics that he'd been using against international communism and the CPA."

"Black-bag jobs," I said wryly.

"And all the rest, everything you're engaged in down there in southern Illinois. Like our colleagues in Chicago, New York, Cleveland, L.A. and all the rest of the country. And we were good at such tactics. We'd perfected them in our hunt for commies. Bugs, infiltration, surveillance, informants, we became experts. But ..."

"Another but," I said.

"But we didn't know what the hell we were getting out of this operation. We just couldn't understand the work product. We didn't know anything about the mobsters — how they talked, worked, lived. Our guys weren't stupid, but they hadn't been trained, they had no personal experience with such people. They couldn't understand what they were hearing on the mikes. The slang and the cussing — some agent's wouldn't even *listen* to such trash talk."

He paused for a deep breath. "Also in the early days we closed up shop and went home at nine or ten o'clock after a long day's work. We had no idea that the mobsters didn't even crank up until after midnight. It was a catch-up game from day one, and we're only now beginning to make some headway."

"And it's mostly because of Bobby."

Fred nodded. "He formed his undercover units all over the country. He chose the agents *he* wanted on his team, and Hoover had to go along. You work more for Bobby than for the director, you know."

"Jesus, Edgar must have shit bullets."

"Hell no, he's been severely constipated ever since. Clyde has to clean him out twice a week."

We laughed so hard we just about messed *our* pants.

"Okay, sounds good, doesn't it? But here's the worm in the soup." Fred took another deep breath and signaled for refills. "The brothers were apparently unaware of their Papa Joe's pre-election arrangement with his mobster pals — mostly Giancana and Costello. Their close relationship went all the way back to Prohibition days when Joe Kennedy was a prominent bootlegger. The old bugger made a fortune. Now he arranged for the mob to help raise campaign funds for Jack's election effort. Crucial states were targeted, and the ground troops went to work. Large sums and truckloads of influence came the way of the Democrats in key cities and states."

"West Virginia, Illinois and Chicago," I suggested.

"And Giancana is loudly claiming — we've got many of his rages on tape — that they had spent enough money and brought enough influence to bear to swing the election to Kennedy."

"So now the Kennedys were expected to pay up; to lay off."

"Exactly. Momo even told the piece of ass he was sharing with Jack what they had done and boasted that her sack mate owed the Outfit for his rocking chair and all the prestige of the White House that he now enjoyed."

I need not tell you how it grieved me to hear such comments about President Kennedy and his women. Remember how Gene Elliot used to unnerve me with such sordid allegations? In this business, however, you can't stay dumb forever. I'd come to know about Sinatra and Lawford, their Hollywood girlfriend Judy Exner and how she had become the go-between for Jack and Momo. Hell, *she* was probably the one who got the president elected.

"And now you're telling me that neither Jack nor Bobby is aware of the debt incurred by their old man. That the mob had expected smooth sailing but Bobby is gearing up to destroy the entire organization from top to bottom?"

Fred slumped in his chair and said, "Ain't it the damndest thing you ever heard? And we've already had more success in the organized crime field than in all previous years added together. Bobby's new Organized Crime Section at Justice and 'The Get Hoffa Squad' have us all running through …"

"But damn it, Fred, almost everything we're getting is illegal! It can't be used." It was the same argument I'd used to no avail on Gene Elliot. "And all these threats, this hatred for the Kennedys ..."

"Okay, first, let me tell you about this legal-illegal problem of yours. I've talked with Gene and I understand your concern. But you weren't here in the early days. Now here's how it all came about." He lit a cigarette and said, "It started with Ike back in 1954 when he authorized Hoover to go around the confusing 'interception and disclosure' law ..."

"The law that prevents investigators from using any information in court that was obtained by illegal means," I said, "such as our unwarranted wire intercepts."

"Right, but exceptions were made for Hoover in 'internal security' cases. Ike finally gave in to the Old Man's obsession with Communists and potential sabotage. In such cases, the Bureau could now bug without court authorization, but still could not use the information as evidence in court. 'Intercept' but not 'disclose.' But as raw data, knowledge of plans and procedures, identities, etc., it was invaluable stuff. In a short time we had more undercover FBI agents in leadership positions in the CPA than the real commies had."

We were laughing but soon grew serious again, and Fred continued. "Of course it's not the same with organized crime. We can't infiltrate their units in the same way. They're all Italian or Sicilian, they speak foreign languages, and they have systems of operation and routines that we know next to nothing about. And all of this can't be learned overnight."

"Wonder if things might be different if we had more Italian or Sicilian agents in the field," I said with as much sarcasm as I thought I could get away with. I thought of the two Italian-American recruits in my training class: two, I counted them. I felt sick at my stomach and told him so, and Fred didn't look so good himself.

"You're still suffering the first-case jitters of an undercover assignment," he said. "It'll get better." But clearly his heart wasn't in this pep talk.

"I don't know if I want it to get better," I said glumly. "I started getting these feelings back during NAC. Fred, in the case of organized crime, I learned nothing I didn't already know, except how little the FBI knew about the Mafia."

"And imagine *our* astonishment when we learned that not only was there an organized group that we had belatedly begun calling the Mafia, that we were wrong, that that wasn't their name at all. And we wouldn't have known anything about *Cosa Nostra* had Valachi not fallen into our laps."

Joseph Valachi, a semi-literate soldier in the New York crime family of Vito Genovese, was serving a life sentence for murder and made a deal with the Justice Department to tell all that he knew in return for lifetime protection while serving his sentence. He revealed the inside structure of the Mafia, or *Cosa Nostra*. He named the twenty-four families throughout the United States, their leaders and the structure of a family. He also revealed the secret blood oath, the law of *omerta*. It was taken by all made men in the induction ceremony. Violate the oath and you die. This was why Valachi now required permanent protection for life.

"The FBI knew none of this. Not only did we not know where the families were located, or who the dons or bosses were, we'd never heard of the *Commissione,* the national crime commission dominated by designated leaders of the families. The Commission makes the rules and arbitrates disputes. They meet in New York City, home of the Five Families. No other city has more than one family."

We fell silent for a time and then Fred ordered drinks. Finally, I said, "And with all this knowledge, why aren't we ..."

"One word — Hoover."

****

And what good was all this knowledge doing me, the country, or anyone? I asked myself a few nights later in my apartment. It was my night off from mike duty, Pattie was already asleep, and my cup runneth over with gin.

The mike talk of late, here and around the country, commingled with our informant acquisitions, was more incendiary than ever. A raging fury toward Bobby was rising because of his treatment of Carlos Marcello who, along with Hoffa, had topped the A.G.'s "Get List" from day one.

Marcello was not an American citizen. He was born in Tunisia, and his parents bought him to the United States as a child. None of this was a secret, and local and federal authorities accommodated him. But after the glare of the Kefauver hearings in the '50s, the don had been required by the Immigration and Naturalization Service to report quarterly in the New Orleans office to support his right to remain in the country. It was all for show, and of course, no adverse ruling was ever forthcoming, and Marcello conducted his business as usual.

Until one day in early April, 1961, a few months after Bobby's appointment as attorney general, when the crusading young avenger struck. Marcello and his lawyer had dutifully reported for his quarterly appearance when a team of immigration agents unceremoniously clapped handcuffs on the Little Man and, over the protests of his lawyer and without a court hearing, he was declared an illegal alien and sentenced to immediate deportation. While protesting in a cornucopia of undecipherable languages, Marcello was escorted to a waiting government plane.

He was first dumped in Guatemala City, then El Salvador and finally Honduras, where he was forced to cross the border on foot and alone. At age fifty-one, overweight and in poor health, still wearing a business suit and tie, he traversed twenty miles or so under the steaming jungle sun before reaching a remote peasant village. He contacted his distraught people in New Orleans. With their help, the infuriated Little Man made his way back to The Big Easy, to The City That Care Forgot, with a heart filled with rage and a throbbing determination for revenge.

I learned later — and I think it is true — that Dave Ferrie flew Marcello home without passing through customs. The government — read the attorney general — was, of course, perplexed and humiliated by the don's sudden reappearance. But infuriated though Bobby and his cohorts may have been, this time matters were handled publicly in a court of law. Marcello was fined hundreds of thousands of dollars for a variety of federal offenses but remained free to go about his business as a salesman of tomato paste.

This scandalous episode was probably the greatest mistake that Robert Kennedy would make in his short life.

I was beginning to unravel. I was a G-man. The kid had lived his dream, at least for a while. But all I did in my limited spare time was drink and stew.

I was no longer the patriotic young government servant. With each morning shave I faced the loss of innocence. Lie, cheat, steal. Just don't get caught and never bad-mouth Hoover — do and your ass was rancid goose liver. I'd always wanted to know everything about everybody, but now I knew too goddamned much about too many people.

But what about all the accomplishments, you ask, the many constructive things you *have* learned. Accomplishments like breaking-and-entering techniques, illegal electronic device installments, identity concealment. No one in the southern part of the state — East St. Louis, Bellville, Carbondale and all the others — knew who we really were or why we were here. All of our activities were covert. Even our personal informants didn't know our real names; some of them didn't even know for sure who we worked for. You could commit any crime, make any mistake, cause any amount of damage, and as long as you didn't embarrass the Bureau there was no personal liability. After all, as the Shadow says: *Nobody knows who you are.*

"And you're so damn good at it, man. People really like you, think well of you, and most importantly, they trust you. You'll make a natural recruiter," Ron Hinchley said one day up in Springfield during one of our unauthorized coffee breaks outside the office.

"The next time I want to be insulted, I'll let you know."

He gave me a penetrating look, then demanded: "Why the hell did you join the Bureau? What did you think it would be like, Dick Tracy to the rescue?"

"I think I've seen more of the Joker."

Life was becoming more Orwellian day by day. We listened to the trash talk on the mikes, broke into a few homes and offices to bug phones, made our reports and watched as little or nothing resulted. One of my informants out of East St. Louis braced me over drinks one night somewhere in this time frame. "Don't you guys take anything seriously?"

"Like what?"

"Like a fuckin' bullet in the head. Like having their homes, kids and dogs all blown to bits. The guys can't be restrained much longer, and with the encouragement they been ..."

"Whoa. What guys? Encouragement from whom? Where and when?"

"You *know* what I'm talkin' about."

I did know, and it was just about to turn my stomach inside out. Ron Hinchley and a couple of my other colleagues were getting the same kind of stuff from some of their informants. And With what I had learned about Operation Mongoose, I sensed that all hell was about to break loose. And with so much money — if it was all true — so much money flowing about, well, the offer couldn't be expected not to be taken up. It wouldn't even take a don and his whole family. A crew or even a single shooter might take the bait. As the poet said, the brothers K "would not live long enough to comb gray hair."

And the covert boys would never even have to surface. I wondered if St. Cloud or Martin were operating as money men on the project. I'd had no contact from either of them for some time. I hinted at this in another talk with Fred Osborn.

"You aren't far off base. You know how the brothers are hated. But Jack is so damned fatalistic — if he's going to go, so be it. And Bobby is a typical crusader with his head in the clouds ..."

"Talking to the Man upstairs, don't you know, getting His blessing."

Fred laughed, but a grimness permeated our talk. If the brothers weren't taking any of this seriously, *we* were. But what good did our concern do? Nobody was listening.

"They're going to get them, Fred. One brother or the other, or both. Mobsters, Hoffa's thugs, Company covert operators ..."

"Or the anti-Castro hot heads in Miami. Jack is making sure they have all the reasons they need. Gonna pull everybody out of Southeast Asia, bring 'em all home. Forfeit billions of corporate dollars in the process. He can't get away with it."

"Ike's warning about the military-industrial complex was on the money," I said, "but he didn't tell the new guy how to handle it and keep his scalp in tact."

Fred belted down his drink and stood up. "Got to go. Important matters to deal with: stolen cars, interstate transportation of gambling paraphernalia, CPA infiltration of local schools and universities. Potential assassinations? Nah."

I stayed and had another martini.

There was no way for me to integrate what my colleagues and I were learning with what was being done by higher authority to make use of all the alarming information. And what was so galling was the consensus that had Papa Joe Kennedy not suffered his debilitating stroke just before Christmas, most of this rising danger could have been resolved through his long-time connections with the wiseguys and his influence over his sons. But all of that potential influence was gone after Joe's illness

Robert Kennedy

PART NINE

Days of Fear and Loathing

What followed was the worst period of my life up to that time. I should have been content. I was a G-man with a closet full of three-piece suits, snap-brim hats, a government car always gassed and at my disposal and monthly paychecks that came on time and never bounced. I had it made.

But I was learning about off-the-book schemes every day that were being fomented by covert operators in other government agencies (occasionally with FBI assistance), faceless ones who aspired to the perpetration of assassinations at home and abroad, the instigation of foreign wars, and the waging of ceaseless black operations. Who the hell were the crooks and gangsters?

And how could such be the case in the greatest democracy in the history of the world? What had happened to us? Where and when had our government gone off course? Surely we weren't always like this. Or had covert action been at the root of all of our national affairs since day-one? I suppose it was possible. After all, our great democratic experience was born out of revolution. Wasn't ours the ultimate coup d'état with Washington, Jefferson and Adams among the greatest of history's conspirators? Had we lost the war with Great Britain, these three and many others would have been hanged as traitors. You can see how I was coming unglued.

But one thing was certain: FBI was not the savior of our constitutional government. The Bureau could not be trusted to fulfill its duty, not as long as J. Edgar Hoover ruled.

Hoover and Tolson had conducted a homosexual relationship, according to my sources at the Bureau, from the earliest days. They partied together, vacationed together two and three times each year at government expense or gratis from intimate friends such as Texas oil men Sid Richardson and Clint Murchison, owner of the Texas Book Depository in Dallas. And they held hands, kissed, and indulged in the intimacies common to lovers. Edgar also partied and vacationed in the company of numerous young men and often with another homosexual and communist-basher, Cardinal Spellman. Agents had either seen Hoover in drag or knew people who had witnessed such performances.

There were photographs, they said, and more than a few solid sources professed to have seen them, including mobsters Frank Costello and Meyer Lansky. And there was the story about Hoover's arrest on a sex charge in New Orleans back in the late twenties, a tale that I'd been told of back in my college days by my Tampa high school friend who was an FBI clerk in the New Orleans field office. The charge was fixed by Carlos Marcello, and Hoover had been beholden to the mob ever since, which helped explain his idiotic attitude toward the non-existence of organized crime.

In addition, Fred Osborn told me that the new CIA director, John McCone, who had taken over after Allen Dulles was fired by JFK for the botched Bay of Pigs adventure, had no authority. Richard Helms, a super-secret egocentric liar ran the Agency, he said, along with its insider legions of covert operators. Helms had been spearheading Agency dirty business for years. Entrenched WAASP influence continued to rule the CIA, especially with Helms in the driver's seat. And now they were in league with "non-existent" Mafia dons and the rabid pack of Cuban exiles out of Miami, Tampa and New Orleans. Their plan was to assassinate Castro and militarily invade Cuba.

"The goddamned CIA has become a rogue elephant," said Fred and ordered us another round of martinis. "Come to think of it, the Agency has probably always been out of control. It began with Truman, emerging out of the wartime OSS. He didn't want them involved in anything but intelligence collection and analysis, certainly not covert paramilitary operations, but he couldn't control them and neither could his successor. Though Ike was a premier spymaster, he didn't even try to rein in the loose canons down in Cockroach Alley — CIA headquarters before the recent construction of the lavish Langley facility."

Fred paused, fished an olive out of his glass and popped it into his mouth. He was clearly uncomfortable but resolved to continue. "And today neither Kennedy trusts the Company; but they can't control it either, witness the debacle at the Bay of Pigs. And now they want to get all U.S. troops out of Southeast Asia and find a way out of the Cold War, while the CIA intends to deepen it. It's a no-win proposition for reasoned thought and conduct."

"Every time we talk I go away more depressed than ever. What the hell are we going to do in this snake pit? Just stand by and watch the disaster to come?"

"That just about says it. Jack won't lay off the cunt he's sharing with Momo, and Bobby won't lay off his prosecutorial crusade against the underworld and Hoffa."

"Jesus, where will it end?"

"I think you know as well as I do."

Winter and early spring of 1962 were a personal disaster for me and, I suppose, for Pattie. We tried; well, Pattie tried. She was her dear, sweet self, but my attention was elsewhere.

It was during this time that I learned more about President Kennedy's poor health condition. A friend of mine from training school stopped by to see me in Carbondale. After Pattie went to bed, we had drinks in the front room.

"I can't use names, but I know this for a fact. The president is not long for this world."

I thought he was referring to all the threats that we were aware of and was stunned when he said, "And the shooters better get him soon, or it will be too late for them."

"What the hell are you talking about?"

He confirmed that the president suffered from Addison's disease, a non-curable adrenal insufficiency, and was gravely ill. He had been taking medication for decades, oral cortisone and injections of Novocain, among a series of other powerful concoctions, most of them illegal. The medicines accounted for his telegenic facial color, a classic symptom of adrenal disease, and enhanced his compulsive womanizing due to all the excess androgens in his system.

My education was in full flower.

I flew to Miami and the bar exam and stayed in the Fontainebleau Hotel.

I wondered if I might see Santo Trafficante among the throng of diners. He was reputed to be part-owner of the hotel and spent a good deal of his time here when in Miami on business and/or to visit his young mistress. His attitude toward sex had always been that man had to work hard and have fun in his life. He was nowhere to be seen but a Tampa friend from way back, Arnold

Rinaldi, was at a corner table alone. He waved to me, and I went over.

After some chit chat, Arnie gave me a hard look and said, "Do you Feebies know *anything* about what's going on down here?"

"My assignment is up north."

"And you don't compare notes? Are you guys asleep? Have you learned nothing after the Bay of Pigs?" He was really agitated.

"Don't beat around the bush, Arnie; what's on your mind?"

"This is private and confidential, right? I'm not gonna wind up called before some investigative committee as one of your fuckin' informants, am I?"

"You know me better than that."

"In this day anything can happen." He took a deep breath. "Georgie, all hell's soon gonna break loose down here."

"Is your uncle still ..."

"Leave him out of this."

"O.K., done. Now go on, give it to me."

"This place has been like a raging wasps' nest ever since the failed invasion. The exiles are determined to go back and will let nothing stop them. Not JFK, not Bobby or Hoover." Our waiter brought my martini and a whiskey sour for Arnold. When he was gone, Arnold continued, "I don't think anybody that matters really wants to stop them. Are you Feebies aware of the arrangement? The exile hot heads, the Mafia, and the fuckin' CIA. JM/WAVE is awash with Company funds."

"What are you saying? Give it to me straight."

"I'm saying Jacko will get his pretty head blown off if he gets in the way."

My understanding was that JM/WAVE was the largest CIA station in the western hemisphere. I already knew that the covert operation, the illegal operation called Operation Mongoose to assassinate Castro and invade Cuba, was also based here at the station. We had picked up some of this info in Illinois, but Arnold's observations were formed right here on the spot. His uncle was a long-time worker in the Trafficante organization, and his wife's brother was still a prisoner in Cuba, having been wounded and captured on the beach in the invasion debacle. The fury, Arnold said, was real, and it was incendiary. This madness had to be stopped.

****

Fred Osborn, was already up on most of the info that I came back with from Miami. "How much information did you get from your pal, the don?"

"I didn't see Santo. And he isn't my pal. I know him but that's as far as it goes."

I hesitated. How much could I tell him and still maintain Arnold's confidentiality? "My primary source knows what he's talking about though. He's connected by blood and says all of this will erupt any day now."

I told him everything that Arnie had said.

And then it was back to work. I had to go down to the Carbondale area, see Pattie, and then commence working the earphones. I found Gene Elliot and the rest of the squad the same, and all the wiseguys were the same too. But I was changing by the minute; I was turning inside out. I kept asking the same question: What was I going to do with my life? I had to find that Great Good Place, that final place of escape.

It wasn't only the trash that I'd learned about J. Edgar, my childhood idol, that was causing me such stress. That was bad enough, sure, but the president and his brother ... did they *know* what they were doing? Did they have any idea what was going on around them?

We knew about JFK and his women, any number of whom could have destroyed his presidency should their relationship hit the news organs. Movie actresses, including Marilyn Monroe; models and chorus girls; nurses; prostitutes and White House clerks and secretaries; all such as these comprised an unending roster of pulchritude. The story was rampant that Jack had to have sex two or three times a day with different partners or else suffer debilitating headaches and an inability to work.

Please, Mr. Khrushchev, would you put those rockets on hold until I can knock off another piece of arse?

All of this brings to mind the details of a later meeting between me and one of my mentors whose judgment I highly respected.

"I'm really glad you could meet with me, Fred."

We'd met this night in a café off the beaten path in Springfield, out by the imposing Lincoln Tomb and Memorial at Oak Ridge Cemetery. Mostly only tourists came out this way. It was not long after our Come-to-Jesus discussion about the covert side of government security and the swampy waters that we were presently treading.

"You sounded pretty desperate on the phone. What's going on?"

I didn't answer for a long moment. "I don't know how much longer I can take this," I finally said.

"I know, I've watched it building. You take too much responsibility, George."

"That's just it — nobody seems responsible. Nothing is being done. We send all the info in, holding nothing back, and I assume the same is happening in Chicago and elsewhere. The Bureau must be running these same kinds of undercover jobs all over the country, anywhere there's an on-going major Mafia operation. But as far as I can tell, none of our take is causing any kind of response on up the line."

He crossed his muscular arms and gave me the G-man stare. "Well, you don't know that, do you, George. Mr. Hoover isn't required to keep you in the picture. You do your job and the rest is out of your hands. Hell, all of this hot-mike blather may be just that — hot air. You know what blowhards these bozos are. Half the time they talk just to hear themselves talk. Besides, I repeat, it's not our worry. We're doing our job out here in the field. Jack Kennedy has the Secret Service to nursemaid him." He laughed. "And to keep the bimbos moving in and out without causing too much congestion."

I didn't even smile. "And if it's more serious than that?"

"Say it. What's eating you?"

"What about our last conversation? Am I just supposed to forget all that 5412 rot that we talked about and just go on about business as usual? What if the same guys are planning to do the same sort of thing to the president now that they did at the Bay of Pigs? The same thing or something a hell of a lot worse? You've heard the talk — the hatred, man. Jesus, Fred, why don't we *do* something? How can Hoover just sit on this? Has he even warned the brothers about the potential dangers they face?"

A deep scowl ravaged his handsome face. "Look, I don't know what the old man's doing about any of this. You know how he feels about the Kennedys, especially the kid brother, our boss." He hesitated and then said forcefully: "And I repeat, none of it pertains to you. It's above your pay level and that's all there is to it. You've heard it before: do your work and go home."

"I'm thinking of doing just that. Wherever home might now be." I'd recently begun to think that Thomas Wolfe might well have been right: maybe none of us could go home again, not after all the filth that we'd rubbed our noses in. Who would know me now? Mama, Sally, my friends from the neighborhood, my former school chums?

Then Fred nailed me. "And what'll you do if you do go home? Sell insurance, stocks and bonds?

We drank coffee for a quiet moment. Then Fred said, "I know you've heard all of this before, but you do have a future with the Bureau. And had you stayed in the Army, well, you know how far you could have gone."

"Yeah," I interrupted, "the jungles of Southeast Asia."

He didn't like this any more than I did. "Look, the director can't last forever. Things will be different then. We can get rid of the ass-kissers and then ..."

"Dream on, Fred. Besides, you know Hoover kicked off years ago. That's why they keep Tolson hanging around; to inflate the rubber replica every morning and keep it seated behind the desk under the FBI flag of Fidelity, Bravery and Integrity."

Fred laughed so hard he almost choked, but I worried that he might choke me.

How could I talk this way to a ranking Bureau executive and hope to get away with it? But I didn't have to worry about Fred. He wasn't a run-of-the-mill suit. He cared more about the work and his men than he did about the toadies at HQ. He wouldn't play the old game. He would talk to me, listen, and although he might very well disagree with me, he wouldn't derail my career. He wanted me to succeed.

"You read my draft report of last week. You can see how it interlocks with what we're getting out of our Chicago taps, where things are really cooking. What do you know, Fred — tell me. Has the Company really made a deal with the mob to assassinate Castro? Is the go-between that ex-FBI agent?"

"Robert Mayhew. Yeah, I think they've put it together." His tone of voice and manner told me that he was not at all pleased about this development.

"What do I do with my report?"

"Burn it."

"Then where will all this go from here, once all the mad dogs have been unleashed? Who will be next?" When he didn't respond, I insisted. "Tell me, damn it! Is it 5412 all over again? All of it covert, off the books, no way to be traced? Is that what's going on?"

Fred was beset by the internal agony of what he knew and what he didn't know. "What I'm going to say now could get me shot if you should divulge a word of it to anybody. We won't ever speak about it again. There's something else going on, off the table. I don't know it all, just the outlines, but it's bad." He paused for a long moment and I feared that he might not continue. "There's something so deep, so profound ... the president, Bobby, and a very few of their most trusted cronies are apparently running another operation. The Bureau's not involved, CIA's not involved. Oh, some individuals, maybe, but not our two agencies as a whole. This is a *military* operation."

"*Military?* I thought 5412 prevented such peacetime military use. Such covert missions are supposed to be run by the Central Intelligence Agency. Shouldn't all of this have been clarified by the experience at the Bay of Pigs?"

"JFK has never forgotten or forgiven our failure at the Bay of Pigs. He's obsessed with Castro and his revolutionary government, and he means to take them out."

"Take them out, how?"

"There's a deep secret plan, run by Bobby and the president personally, to invade Cuba. It's on, the day is set. I don't know the precise date but …"

"*Invade* Cuba?" I literally exploded. "How can they …?"

"They have a high-placed mole inside the Cuban government. He's ready and waiting to lead an internal coup. They're really going to do this, George, and it has nothing to do with the Company's link-up with the mob to assassinate Fidel. That's a separate operation."

"How do you know all of this?"

"I've already told you far too much, and if I answered your question I might just as well go on and sign our death warrants. We're on shaky enough ground as it is."

That pretty much ended our conversation. Fred paid the check, got up and wished me luck on the bar exam.

In my darkest moments, one thought always shone through: Jack and Bobby would never be caught asleep at the switch again by those gray-suited bastards who fouled the waters at the Bay of Pigs. That disaster had served as their baptism of political fire. The brothers wouldn't be blindsided again with their guard down. But if what Fred said was true ...?

That conversation took place in 1962, but I remember it as though it had been yesterday. Today I realize that Fred had only known the rudiments of the plan that was being organized.

Self-doubt was rampant; self-respect had been lost perhaps never to be found again.

When I heard I passed the bar, I had one last meeting with Fred before I officially left the Bureau. It was our most significant. We met in Springfield according to our custom, late at night in an out-of-the-way diner on the fringes of the city; catfish, fries, hushpuppies, and extra dry martinis.

"You all packed?"

"Just about. Actually, I've been ready for weeks."

"Pattie riding down with you?"

"Already gone, by bus. We thought it best, as I may stop off in New Orleans."

Fred gave me a look and then shot one in low and hard. "Have you ever heard of the CFR?"

What the hell, I thought. Where was *this* going? "Commission of Foreign Relations," I said.

"Counsel on Foreign Relations."

"Whatever, I don't know much about them. All big shots; government and industry types, according to what little I know."

He nodded and sipped at his drink. "Most powerful men, and a few women, in the country, in the world even. They come from all walks of life, inside government and out. And you *need* to know about them, George. Make it your business to learn as much as you can."

"What the hell for?" I was really perplexed.

"So you can understand where all those guys are coming from and why."

"What guys? What …?"

"Guys like that Martin fellow, and the fop with the three-piece Seville Row suits."

Jesus Christ, how much does he know about my life? And what did it all mean? Now I was really beginning to squirm; I could feel the agitation down in my toes.

"Look, there's just no telling how it's all going to play out. The mob hates JFK and Bobby, mostly the kid and his self-righteous prosecutorial zeal. And the brothers don't help a bit. They're so damned arrogant and headstrong. There are ways of doing things.

"But these young punks, they've been advised and warned, and they just won't listen. They have their own agenda. You know how it heated up after the Bay of Pigs." He paused again and then said, "Hell yes, you want another drink. I damned sure do. This is going to be heavy, kid. I wish … I wish you didn't have to know all of this, but I think I owe it to you before you reenter the world at large."

He signaled our waitress, ordered more drinks and coffee and then said, "You're going to need this one."

I don't think I've ever forgotten a word of what he said that night, and I've seen it proved out so many times in the following years. This is the way I remember it.

It had started during World War I. Hell, it probably started in antiquity days, but I'm going to concentrate on our time. The concept of a one-world community became centered in the CFR just after the war to end all wars was concluded. Already plans for future wars in the furtherance of international trade and the formation of a general association of nations had been laid. In other words, one-world government was their mission.

The membership in the U.S. branch of the CFR consisted of the most powerful and distinguished nabobs in finance, commerce, communications, academia and covert intelligence operations. Yale University was the breeding ground. Skull and Bones Yalies, they were, almost to a man. And the few women members were all connected to the Bonesmen as wives, mistresses or business associates. And here's the most crucial fact — it was all secret. Like the Mafia, the counsel had their own code of *omerta*.

Prominent members of the government, including many of our presidents, held dual leadership positions in the CFR, Fred explained. And all of this activity and secrecy was protected by the national and international news media. Military leaders, officers of the departments of State and Defense, and most all CIA directors have also been members of the Counsel.

All of this and more came at me like a dose of salts, and I was stunned. The guy who had always wanted to know *everything,* who believed there was no such thing as too much knowledge, was now on the edge of overload.

"What about Hoover?" I asked when I finally located my voice.

"As far as I know, he cooperates but is not a member. You know how he wants to do everything on his own." Fred grinned. "Now I know what you're thinking. Why don't they get rid of him? But in his secret files he has it all, every detail about the Counsel's make-up, the membership and its mission. Not to mention detailed information on each member's sins and foibles, with which he could blow them out of the water. It's the same way that he keeps presidents and congressmen under his polished thumb nails. They've all decided to accept cooperation and just wait for nature to take their side. After all, the man is bound to die in the next hundred years or so."

I didn't even laugh. "And why exactly are you telling me all of this?" I asked with the heavy expectation that he was quite prepared to tell me why.

"Those guys, all the recruiters breathing down your neck, and other targets like you, will swarm when you reenter the private sector. So you must remember at all times that all of them are either members or are CFR-controlled. And the few who aren't are controlled by others who are and who don't always know *who* they really work for. The leadership, however, is a hundred percent corrupt and self-interested."

I hardly slept that night. Later that morning I was parked on the street near the office while I checked out for the last time. I said goodbye to everyone, and Fred Osborn walked me out to the car and actually held the door for me.

"It's a good decision, George; you're making the right move. Now be careful, don't get sucked back into this wretched way of life. No matter what part of the alphabet makes the pitch, it will suck you dry, down to the marrow of your being, down to your very soul."

He reached into the window, grabbed my shoulder and shook me hard with unconcealed emotion. "I wish *I'd* had such advice when I was young and there was still time for me. Now get out, George, get out and stay out!"

Wow, *that* was a surprise.

I would start over again with a stopover in New Orleans.

****

New Orleans. The City That Care Forgot, the hotbed of my coming of age experiences.

I phoned one of my old Chicago buddies who had continued to live here after graduation and his military tour of duty. He had become a successful businessman with a beautiful wife but no children. I will refer to him hereafter as Rob Merritt. We met at a restaurant on Magazine Street in the Garden District, and it was like old times.

"Damn," he said, "you look just the same, still the all-American kid."

"Your eyesight has seriously weakened, along with your memory cells."

We laughed and ordered lunch: soup, oysters on the half-shell and beer for me. "Not quite like the old days," I noted, as Rob had ordered iced tea with his food.

"Doctors say I have to lay off the booze."

"You look good."

"Better every day." He sipped his tea and then said, "Now what are you doing here? I saw Bill Ferlita just before he moved back to Tampa, and he said you had become one of Hoover's boys. You're not gonna slap the cuffs on me, are you?"

"I'm a free man now, no badge and no cuffs. I can do as I please. Why, I may even stay here at Loyola for my fifth year of eligibility."

We cracked up and then Rob said, "So, an attack of nostalgia drew you back?"

"Something like that." I looked cautiously around the room, but it was well past the normal lunch hours, and the restaurant was not crowded. "You've had a considerable success in the last few years, so you must have had your ear close to the ground."

He gave me a hard look and said, "You sure you're an *ex*-Feebie?"

I nodded. "No wires, no one to report to, and no names ever to be used."

He remained cautious and checked the room too, and when he felt secure he began to open up. "Yeah, I've watched and listened. And you remember what it's like here — to succeed you deal with all sorts. I think I know the kind of things you want to hear."

Our waitress came and left, and we began to eat. The food was excellent.

"I was back in Tampa," I said, "finishing my last year of law school when the fiasco at the Bay of Pigs erupted."

"This place was like a chapter out of *Alice in Wonderland*. You probably know that a lot of the preliminary work and planning for the invasion was done here. Training camps across the river and all through the bayous. Guns, ammo and materials were collected, shipped in from Dallas, and stored here prior to shipment down your way. All done out of offices right here in the Crescent City."

"And all done in public view, I suppose."

"Yep. Citizens, law enforcement agents, spooks — your kind — and a horde of Castro-haters and sympathizers hard at work."

"Someone had to be in control. Who was the honcho?"

"You remember a guy by the name of Banister?"

"Guy Banister? Hell yes I remember him: FBI, ONI and a CIA background."

"That's the guy. Ran the whole damned show from his office over on Camp Street. All of it hidden in plain sight."

"Camp Street. I seem to remember …"

"You got it, located right across the street from offices of the FBI, CIA, Secret Service and ONI. Not exactly a prime site for covert operations. Unless …"

"Unless it was a protected venture."

"That's it. Place was swarming with revolutionaries. New recruits in and out for indoctrination and training, armed Cubans in fatigues coming and going, weapons crates moving through the building day and night. David Ferrie, Marcello's private pilot-on-call, was always there. Remember him, said to be the guy who rescued Carlos out of the swamps of Central America in RFK's botched attempt to extradite him?"

I nodded. Sure, I remembered Ferrie. How could you forget such a ghoul? I'd heard that he was completely bald now from severe alopecia and wore a reddish toupee and unmatched greasepaint eyebrows. He was a bright man and had never met a subject he didn't consider himself an expert on.

"He was an important cog in the operation. I often saw him dressed in fatigues and combat boots, bossing all the Cubans around while they loaded the weapons crates onto trucks for transport out to the air field. A great pilot, you know, made regular cargo flights down to Miami, Guatemala and other points south. But Banister was the boss."

"And you saw some of this with your own eyes?"

"I often stopped for breakfast at Mancuso's downstairs around the corner from the offices of 544 Camp Street. Man, it was all wide open, no secrets. Even Clay Shaw was there occasionally, not working but conferring privately with Banister. You remember him, founder of the Trade Mart, busy lecher about town."

"Yeah, I remember Shaw. Used to call himself Clay Bertrand."

"That's him," Rob said. "And the whole damned thing was for nothing, George. You must know this. Castro knew it all and was ready and waiting from day one. He had as many sympathetic spies here as our side had eager revolutionaries and would-be assassins. Many of the invasion team were dead ducks before they knew what hit them. The others are prisoners and who knows what ordeals they have experienced? Cuban prisons aren't rehab clinics."

"Some of my friends in Tampa know what they experienced, and I don't think they'll ever forget or forgive."
"And many of the Cubans killed and captured were from New Orleans. Their friends and families won't forget anytime soon either. Believe me when I say it, they hate your ex-bosses with a passion, maybe more than they hate Castro. But I guess you Feebies know that, right?"

"*They* know. Remember, I'm now a private citizen."

"Well, what are *they* doing about it?"

I shrugged glumly and pushed away from my plate. What could I say? I'd been asking myself the same question for months. In any case, Rob didn't wait for an answer.

He took aim and nailed me right between the eyes.

"They're going to be hit, Georgie. Don't know when or where, and I don't know who will do the deed. But the brothers will be hit before JFK can run for reelection." He paused and then said meaningfully, "And there will never be a Kennedy dynasty."

Bobby, too? I was shaken to the core. This was exactly what some of my former Bureau colleagues and I had feared for so long. We left the restaurant and stood on the sidewalk nearby. "I've shot my mouth off enough," Rob said. "It's good to see you, kid, but hanging out with you is potentially dangerous to the health."

"I keep telling you that I'm no longer ..."

"I don't care what *you* tell me. Now *this* is it, buddy: two names. Go to the library and look up their current activities." He scribbled the names on a folded napkin and shook my hand. "Take care and don't linger too long in this town. It's *not* your home anymore. Not now, not for a very long time. Maybe never again."

I watched him walk away and then drove over to the library on St. Charles Avenue.

I remembered all the hours spent here rather than in the library at school with my class books. I remembered the leather sofa, the books and the discovery of what I really wanted to do with my life. Maybe now, at long last, I could get about the work that had been calling to me for so long.

That night I stayed at a boarding house farther up on the avenue, and the next afternoon I met Frank Klein at a coffee shop in the French Quarter.

"Thanks for coming on such short notice, Frank."

"I'm pleased to have a chance to see you. You left school so unexpectedly, I always wondered what happened to you. Didn't you have another year of eligibility?"

"That's why I'm here. I'm gonna claim ..."

That got us laughing. Frank's name was one that Rob had given me, along with that of Jim Garrison. At the library I had learned that Garrison was the newly elected district attorney in Orleans Parish, and Frank was his chief assistant. They'd worked together from the time that Garrison was an assistant D.A. Garrison had married one of my college friends, and they were busily producing kids like oven biscuits.

"From newspaper reports it would seem that Big Jim's doing a fine job."

"He's making his mark."

Frank was careful in what he said. I sensed that I wouldn't get much out of him on the matters that Rob and I had discussed. His Teutonic self-discipline was as strong as it had been in our college days, and now he was a government official with duties and responsibilities that prevented loose talk.

"Yes, in answer to your unasked question, it was busy here in those days. A lot of preparation had to be done for the invasion, and a good bit of it was done right here. And before you ask, yes, we knew what was going on. I don't think Jim would have put up with it, but he wasn't the D.A. then. Cubans were everywhere, anti-Castro hotheads and Castro supporters. Lots of fighting, not much accomplished. You remember Boogie?"

"Murret," I said, "basketball and baseball. Nice guy."

"Do you remember his cousin, the scrawny kid that was always hanging around?"

"Vaguely, but I never spent any real time with him. Why?"

"Name was Lee Harvey Oswald. Grew up in the Murret home in the midst of some of the worst underworld joints in the city, most of which were owned by Marcello. The father and uncle, Dutz Murret, was one of Marcello's loan sharks. Not a particularly bad sort, but he was trapped in his way of life like most of the low-level workers. The kid's divorced mother ran around with an assortment of local wiseguys, and Lee grew up pretty much unsupervised."

Frank filled me in on Oswald's bio. In 1955, while still in high school, Oswald began attending meetings of the Civil Air Patrol, where David Ferrie was his supervisor. I remembered having seen them there during my college days. Oswald, Frank said, was smart enough but almost as bizarre as Ferrie. He dropped out of school and in late 1956 joined the Marines. He became a radar specialist and was eventually assigned to a base in Japan. There he was schooled for some vague reason in the Russian language. Oh, and his cousin — the one alleged to be an officer with CIA — was also in Atsugi at that time."

"Were they working together?"

"We don't know. Most of her comings and goings are blurred by smoke and mirrors. What we do know is that in 1960, Oswald received a hardship discharge on the grounds that his ailing mother needed him. But he didn't come home. One way or another he got himself into the Soviet Union and relinquished his passport. Locals were surprised to learn he was a foreigner, since he spoke such good Russian. He met and married a Russian girl, a niece of a Soviet officer in MKV, eventually had his passport returned with no questions asked and, with his wife and child, flew back to America on money borrowed at the U.S. Embassy."

He paused and then asked, "Any of that raise a stink under your nose?"

I nodded. "What's the accepted explanation?"

"It was all a setup, arranged from beginning to end, maybe with collusion from both sides. For what reasons, *that's* what we still don't know."

"He's a government agent, maybe an informant for one agency or another. Is that what you're saying?"

He didn't respond and we fell silent for a time. I didn't know what to ask, and that gave Frank time to decide how far he wanted to go with all of this.

"The next thing *we* know about him is when he showed up back here in New Orleans with his growing family. Still obnoxious, he was arrested one day down on Canal Street while handing out leaflets in support of Castro. He was attacked by a bunch of anti-Castro patriots, they all got into a scuffle — real or phony, take your pick — and finally some of them were arrested, Oswald included."

"Go on," I said, "you're leading up to something."

"Printed on the leaflets was the address of the Fair Play for Cuba association headquartered here in New Orleans." He pierced me with those ice-blue eyes and said, "The address was the same as Guy Banister's detective agency at 544 Camp Street."

* * * * * * * * * * * * * *

Tampa, Florida; home sweet home. Pattie and I moved into an apartment out near Dale Mabry Avenue and the exclusive Holiday Inn Hotel and Restaurant.

I went to work in one of the most prominent law firms in Florida. I had clerked for this firm in my last year of law school, and they were eager to have me back. It was a promising start as I attempted to ease into the practice of law, but I knew from the first day that it wasn't what I wanted or needed.

It grieves me to acknowledge that I began to respond to the warm attentions bestowed on me by secretaries in ours and other law firms, along with a bevy of accommodating clerks and judicial secretaries at the courthouse. I was not untroubled by these developments, however pleasant they were in the moment.

Still, I reasoned that if this sort of thing was acceptable by the president and attorney general, by two-thirds of the White House administration, and by the keeper of all morals and ethical conduct, J. Edgar Hoover — or J. Edna, as many called him — then maybe it was good enough for me.

Many of my Bureau colleagues and I had known about Jack Kennedy's affair with Judy Exner, the beautiful California model he was sharing with mobsters Sam Giancana and Johnny Roselli; whom White House secretaries referred to as Twiddle and Twaddle; and, of course, the numerous Hollywood starlets, primarily Angie Dickenson and the goddess of sex, Marilyn Monroe. And there were said to be nude swimming frolics almost daily in the White House pool, at least when Jackie was out of town. I never personally witnessed any of this or participated, but the details were clear and explicit.

After word slipped out about Exner's pregnancy by the president and Giancana's role in arranging her abortion, matters took a sudden turn. This was the incident that ended their affair and could easily have ended Kennedy's presidency. Even *he* had sense enough to realize how close to the edge he was skating, and there was no alternative. The collusive arrangement was ended. JFK wasn't too upset; after all, there was a legion of substitutes waiting in the wings.

But women were not the only concerns in that hot summer of '62. President Kennedy was not particularly worried about all the strum and drang raised in Berlin the previous year by the Soviet construction of the wall in East Berlin, but he was concerned with Vietnam and Cuba. He dispatched thousands of "advisers" to assist the South Vietnamese combat units, many of whom were killed in battle, all with little publicity. Tragic, yes, but Kennedy was determined not to lose Vietnam to the Communists.

Accordingly, he supported CIA covert operations, actions that included the use of U.S. aircraft in the spraying of virulent herbicide defoliants in jungle areas where the Viet Cong were thought to be operating. This was in direct violation of the Geneva Accords of 1954. President Kennedy, however, agreed with his vocal military commanders that the action in Vietnam was a "military affair" and was beyond the restrictions of the Geneva Accords.

And there was Fidel Castro to contend with. We had a score to settle with the "bearded one." The Kennedys and the United States had been humiliated at the Bay of Pigs, and the disgrace would not be allowed to stand. Early in the new year of 1962, Operation Mongoose had been officially launched. It would continue uselessly for some while, but in the meantime the Kennedys, the media, and the public's attention was drawn back to more personal concerns.

On August 4, 1962, the magnificent physical specimen sung the memorable "Happy Birthday, Mr. President" at Jack Kennedy's 45th birthday party, and had been making presidential news ever since.

Marilyn Monroe and Jack had been lovers since the early 1950s, and after Jack's election in 1960 the affair began to spiral out of control. By 1962, a longtime battle with narcotics and excessive drinking had Marilyn in a tailspin. Jack shouldn't even have looked at her, let alone closeted himself with her for private time. Marilyn irrationally believed that she truly loved Jack and wanted him to divorce Jackie and marry her. Upon his rejections she would often explode in vicious tirades and threaten to expose their relationship. The affair just had to end badly.

Hoover could have blown Kennedy's career to dust. He knew all about Kennedy's women, not just Marilyn. And as with Judy Exner, Edgar knew all about Marilyn's pregnancy by Jack and her abortion in Mexico, which was arranged again by the accommodating Momo Giancana. Only Jack, Bobby and father Joseph Kennedy's awareness of his homosexuality kept the imperious FBI director in line.

Finally Jack cut the cord with Marilyn and dispatched Bobby to handle the deed. Marilyn hit bottom, and her depression and despair promised to lead to even more trouble. Bobby did his best to console her, but Marilyn had other ideas about her recovery needs. At brother-in-law Peter Lawford's house in Malibu, the scene of many of her previous trysts with Jack, Bobby dutifully became her lover. The affair overheated. Marilyn was so ripped by constant drink and drugs that she could scarcely tell the difference between the brothers. Now she insisted on *their* marriage and, because of Bobby's resistance, she sank into a deep psychic collapse.

May 19, 1962:   President John F. Kennedy (back to the camera), Attorney General Robert Kennedy (far left), and Marilyn Monroe, on the occasion of President Kennedy's 45th birthday celebrations at Madison Square Garden. Arthur Schleslinger appears at far right and Harry Belafonte in Rear.

Bobby panicked. To make matters worse, every detail of the affair was captured by bugs and camera devices throughout the Lawford house. Edgar, the CIA and the mob all collected the dirty evidence in their secret files.

Come the 4th of August, the script had reached The End, but there would be no cinematic fade out. Marilyn was found dead by her housekeeper, the victim of an overdose of self-administered barbiturates. At least that was the public story. But all the evidence indicates that Marilyn was murdered.

Robert Kennedy and Peter Lawford, responding to frantic calls from Marilyn's housekeeper, returned from Malibu to Marilyn's house that night and found her naked in bed, either dead or dying. An ambulance was called, and half way to the hospital, when it was clear that she was already dead, the ambulance turned around, her body was returned to her bedroom, and doctors were summoned to the scene.

Bobby returned to his normal schedule far away from the drama unfolding in Los Angeles. Utter terror must have raced through the Kennedy brothers and all involved in the cover-up when it was publicly announced by police that Robert Kennedy had been in her home when Marilyn died and that a wadded piece of paper had been found under her bed with the White House phone number scribbled on it!

The Kennedy brothers immediately began publicly praising FBI Director J. Edgar Hoover for all of his years of conscientious and dedicated service to law and order, world peace, and the demise of Communism. What the hell was going on?

Well, soon thereafter it was learned that not a single photo of Marilyn with either brother existed in the photo agency file of the FBI.

I had considered myself free of all such garbage. That's why I was in Tampa, but life so often turns left just when you think you're going right.

During this time, there remained an unbridgeable gap between Pattie's and my outlook on life. I was a lawyer in a prominent law firm, and she worked in a major accounting office. She loved the potential of our life together, while I was already thinking about how we could move on.

Shortly before I'd left Springfield on my return to Tampa, a couple of second-class scandal sheets had published the story that John Kennedy had been previously married, albeit briefly, when he was a young man. The first wife was identified as a Florida socialite named Durie Malcolm. The Kennedys denied the claim, and father Joe was alleged to have had all traces of the union removed from court records. No sign of a divorce ever materialized, and the unsubstantiated claim arose that Jack's marriage to Jackie was bigamous.

I'd paid little attention to the reports back then as my focus was on my resignation from the Bureau and my inevitable return to Tampa. The story had finally been debunked in *Newsweek* with the covert research assistance of J. Edgar Hoover. Once more into the breach and how he must have rejoiced at having the Kennedy family once again in his debt. But it was too late. The story had seeded and taken hold. In Tampa that summer, the scandalous rumor was once again out and about.

"Yeah, it's hot stuff again," said Johnny Hicks one day at the Palma Ceia Country Club over lunch. He was an associate with a big Tampa firm and had once practiced law as a younger man in Spalding County. "They were married in 1947 down in Palm Beach, no secret about it. The old man went bonkers. He was already grooming Jack to run for president and here the kid was cutting his own throat on the public gallows. Well, Joe got everything taken care of, no paper trace left in the Spalding County Courthouse in Palm Beach. Remember, the Kennedys live down there and know how to operate."

"Do you know all of this for certain, or are you just passing on more of the anti-Kennedy slop?"

"I have a dozen reliable informants in Spalding County."

It presented a hellacious prospect. If this scandalous story got traction it could blow JFK right out of the water well before the '64 reelection campaign.

August had indeed been a wretched month.

But then in September and early October the president and the attorney general had to confront the incendiary racial uproar on the campus of Ole Miss University. The school administration and the governor of the state had refused to allow one black student to enroll at the university. Federal marshals were sent in to see that it was accomplished peacefully according to court order.

But the confrontation escalated, and the president sent in federal troops and a reluctant FBI to combat the violence. Hoover resisted almost as much as the racist governor, but in the end, James Meredith had been enrolled and the violence curtailed.

Then, suddenly, all attention was focused on mass survival when the Cuban Misssle Crisis erupted in mid-October, threatening the destruction of mankind and all those wonderful places so attractive to me. Our spy planes had detected Soviet construction teams working on surface-to-air missile launch sites in Cuba. With these missile sites in operation, the Soviets could reach almost every nook and cranny in the continental U.S.A. The world had never come so close to total annihilation.

On October 22, Kennedy announced a blockade around the island of Cuba with almost full support from the American people and the Organization of American States. Kennedy's response in

Nikita Khrushchev and President Kennedy

the face of so much opposing advice was masterful. Most of his administrative staff, the Joint Chief's and a mouth-frothing horde of right-wing politicians advocated the immediate obliteration of Cuba, and should the Soviet Union so much as make a gesture in our direction they should be blitzed as well. And we later learned that Chairman Khrushchev was being battered by the same kind of pressure by his hardliners. But Kennedy and Khrushchev held firm, and in all likelihood saved mankind from incineration.

The blockade ended after thirteen days and the Soviets sent no further supplies. All of their supply ships turned back at the blockade line, literally at the last moment. Secretary of State Dean Rusk put it this way: "We're eyeball to eyeball, and I think the other guy just blinked."

But Kennedy had as many detractors as grateful supporters of his performance. He caught hell for perceived cowardice from many of our political, military, and intelligence officials, and most members of his cabinet, Lyndon Johnson and Dean Rusk included.

They openly wanted us to incinerate the island of Cuba and dare the Soviets to react.

My God, I thought, more internal hatred of the brothers. It seemed to me that a season of madness had enveloped the entire country.

"If you're not watching, turn on the TV, quick!" It was a Nixon supporter in the recent election calling from our law office, but I was already watching the incredible spectacle down in Miami.

I'd been talking about the upcoming event with a few of my former Bureau associates now posted to the Tampa Bay region. My best contact — I'll call him Danny McNight — was a New Yorker assigned down south. We had met recently at an agreed time and place on the Gulf coast this side of Sarasota. Our conversation that day went something like this:

"How are you, Danny Boy?"

"Fine and dandy-O. My mother's only son, my father's pride and joy."

We ordered and then got down to the reason for our meeting.

"It's absolutely incredible. Don't they listen?" he said. "Don't they pay attention to *anything* we tell them? Or is the Hoov keeping it all under wraps, and the brothers don't have any idea how bad things are getting?"

"Don't ask me. You're still on the firing line; I'm a private citizen with bills to pay and a government to trust in. What's the latest? Tell it to me straight."

His facial expression visibly hardened. "They'll be waiting for him in the Orange Bowl, gunning for him. Most of his advisers don't want him to go; they're worried that he'll be booed in such a hostile environment."

"Booed? What the bloody hell? They'll blow his head off."

"But Bobby insists that he go. The country needs it, he says, Cuban-American relations need it, and most of all Jack needs it. It's well known in the inner circles that the president was ripped by the catastrophe at the Bay. He knows he couldn't have legally sent in American military forces under the restraints of 5412, but his enormous self-guilt had been eating him up."

"Why self-guilt? Why not place the blame where it belongs?"

"He's pissed with himself for having listened to the fuck-heads at CIA. That's why he's gonna wipe 'em out when he's reelected."

"If he lives to be reelected."

"You got it. Many outings like this goddamn Orange Bowl caper ..."

"You said they'll be waiting."

He nodded. "We already have word that would-be assassins are being readied for the big event. They'll be there, George. JFK will be at risk from the moment he pulls up in his gleaming convertible. And if he makes it to the podium ..."

"Well, the Secret Service can't let him go! Do they know?"

He shrugged. "Who knows what they know and what they're doing? That's why they are called a *secret* service."

Back in early December, the administration had brokered a deal with Cuba to exchange more than $53 million worth of pharmaceuticals, bulldozers, food and other goods in return for the release of the imprisoned Cuban freedom fighters captured at the Bay of Pigs. Now, on December 29, the president and first lady were appearing before some 50,000 exuberant spectators in Miami at the Orange Bowl to welcome home the released members of Brigade 2506.

Jackie addressed the crowd in fluent Spanish, and then JFK came to the podium where he was presented with the rebels' brigade flag that had been hidden during their confinement. Kennedy said in a high state of emotion, "Commander, I can assure you that this flag will be returned to this brigade in a free Havana."

Pandemonium swept the stadium, many of the released prisoners broke down and wept, and even President Kennedy had tears in his eyes. He later claimed that it was the proudest moment so far of his time in office.

"Yes, I'm watching," I told my law associate on the phone as shouts of *"Guerra! Guerra!"* and *"Libertad!"* erupted from the throng of ecstatic spectators. "It's absolutely astonishing. The man has just publicly declared war on Cuba. Castro will go ballistic!"

Later in the day, I spoke again with Danny McNight, this time on pay phones.

"He was there, Georgie, the would-be assassin. We had his description — a young Cuban male of muscular build — carrying a duffle bag bearing a disassembled scoped rifle. Miami police and Secret Service agents were also on the scent, but the guy couldn't be singled out in that roiling swamp of lookalikes. And the story we got later was that he couldn't get a good vantage point from which to assemble his weapon and fire. The search is still on, but he hasn't been caught so far. No telling where he'll show up next."

A few days after the Miami bowl event, JFK met with reporters and, having realized his unintentional mistake concerning return of the flag, he assured them and the world that the U.S. had no intention of launching a military invasion against Cuba. His statement was intended to reassure Khrushchev and Castro but at the same time it set off a violent rage throughout the Cuban exile community. Kennedy gave and he took away, they said. His name became synonymous with treason. The shadow world of exiles, mobsters and covert government operators renewed their initiative of revenge.

And it wasn't only Cuban exile hotheads whose bile Kennedy had raised. Almost to a man, his cabinet was infuriated with such squeamishness. It was no longer only the Soviets, Cuba and the exiles who were so alienated; it might well be his own government that Kennedy should fear most. There was virtually a coup atmosphere circulating at the highest levels of the administration. The Joint Chiefs of Staff and the intelligence community no longer saw Soviet Russia and Cuba as the primary enemy; rather they focused on the Kennedy brothers, especially the detested attorney general.

These covert commandos prepared their own plans for "success." A top secret memo that later surfaced, signed by our leading military commanders, urged the president to authorize the staging of a series of contrived incidents designed to establish a rational for the invasion of Cuba. These incidents would include faked attacks against U.S. forces at our base in Guantanamo and attacks against Latin American nations throughout the region, all blaming the Cuban government for the flagrant actions.

We would simulate Cuban shoot-downs of American aircraft, civilian and military, and draft phony casualty lists. An American ship in Guantanamo Bay would be blown up, again with the blame placed squarely on Cuba.

The most outrageous of the proposals is enough to make one's blood boil even now. The chiefs suggested that in a venture code named Operation Northwoods, in Miami and other Florida cities and as far north as Washington D.C., a terror campaign would be launched that would result in an international outcry against the Cuban regime.

The plan was to target Cuban refugees in America, blowing up cars and houses with carefully placed plastic bombs, even wounding some individuals, with the blame being laid right at Fidel Castro's door. There was no explanation as to how the perpetrators would limit the injuries only to Cuban exiles in this country and not include innocent American bystanders and Cuban citizens legally living here.

The chiefs were enthusiastic about the plan and when the public animosity against Castro and the Cuban warmongers was raised to fever pitch, they said we would simply — in Air Force Chief of Staff General Curtis LeMay's parlance — "fry the bastards."

Thankfully, higher authority rebuffed the proposed operation, and Secretary of Defense McNamara claimed that he'd never even seen the despicable memo. It was well-known that McNamara and General Lyman Lemnitzer, Chairman of the Joint Chiefs, detested each other, as did JFK and LeMay. It is said that after the Bay of Pigs fiasco, the general actually called President Kennedy a traitor to his face, and Kennedy gave standing orders never to allow LeMay to be alone in his presence again.

The president also considered Lemnitzer an imbecile and made no secret of his feelings. Lemnitzer sent another memo to McNamara insisting "that the Cuban problem be solved in the near future." Now a public document, it went on to inform the Secretary of Defense that the entire Joint Chiefs of Staff unanimously recommended that a national policy of military intervention in Cuba be proclaimed by the president. This was too much. President

Kennedy replaced General Lemnitzer as Chairman of the JCS and inserted his choice of General Maxwell Taylor.

In addition, the administration had to worry about war on the international front and simultaneous resistance to its policies internally. When the CIA, with warmonger Richard Helms in charge, realized that the president was not going to wage war on Cuba with covert CIA support, the Company, without JFK's awareness, simply reinstituted the previous arrangement with its Mafia friends to assassinate Castro, a deed they believed would lead to a U.S. invasion.

Looking back, one feels that filmmaker Woody Allen must have taken charge of the upcoming production of poison pills, long-range telescopic rifles, infected diving suits and other such simple-minded idiocy designed by Company experts to eliminate Castro.

"Have you heard, it's started again?" said Danny McNight over my office phone.

"Yeah, I've talked to some people here. But they assure me that Santo is not involved this time."

"He's not, nor is Giancana. This time they're relying on Johnny Roselli and that mental case down at JM/WAVE ..."

"Bill Harvey," I said and felt the bile rise in my throat.

"And he's more locked and loaded than ever before." I knew there was more on the way. "He's already assembled a crew of Agency full-time assassins. And this time, who knows whose head may get shredded?"

✳✳✳✳✳✳✳✳✳✳✳✳✳✳

The recent ordeal of the missile crisis had focused the public's attention. Business as usual was more difficult to maintain with any degree of aplomb. The nation was flat out terrorized by fear of strontium 90, the radioactive fallout from all of the nuclear tests, ours and Russia's, that were verifiably polluting the atmosphere. Even the recent test ban treaty had had little positive effect in slowing the depraved arms race. Both nations would make ameliorating noises and continue testing underground.

Citizens had, I thought, to do whatever they could to save mankind. Self-deluded poppycock? With hindsight, probably so; but at the time ...

I passed on whatever information I possessed and what I was learning since having returned to the Florida hive. I made anonymous alarm calls to the local FBI office, a former colleague in Illinois, and two or three active agents in RA's along the Gulf Coast, and to local newsmen and whatever supreme powers were listening.

I rang a few bells.

My downhill slide began with two female informants, unofficial to be sure. They were calling me for phone sex, and it was only later that I realized that someone was recording the calls.

"I hear you're looking for information." I'd heard that one before and hung up.

"Who was that?" Pattie asked while getting ready for bed.

"Wrong number."

Often Pattie caught the bus to work before I had to leave for the office. My schedule was pretty much my own, unless there was a court hearing or trial to attend.

"Why do you hang up," said the now familiar voice one morning. "I told you I can give you what you want, and you can give me ..."

I hung up.

There were two or three others, steamier and more persistent. Eventually, I thought I recognized one of the voices and began to develop the conversation. But no important information was forthcoming beyond the growing sexual explicitness.

Occasionally, information came my way that I would pass along to Danny and a few of the others. I only met with a couple of these hot numbers, however, and mostly it was all just steamy talk. Jesus, the female of the species, I remember thinking.

God, I loved them so.

"How the hell do you get this kind of info, even the occasional name?" Danny McNight and I were rehashing events over my gin and his sour mash. It was springtime, hot and humid, and we were seated on the terrace of one of our favorite watering holes overlooking the Hillsborough River. "It can't just be courthouse gossip, or cocktail party talk."

"It's all over town. Ybor's buzzing day and night, probably worse in Miami, and you can just imagine the scene over on Bourbon Street."

"Well, whatever, maybe you ought to cool it a little. Remember, there's no badge backing up your snooping intrusions these days. You're on your own. And you damn sure can't use *my* name to help you out of a scrape. In a situation like that, I never heard of you. I mean, hell, you're a good buddy and I appreciate our talks. But you're not one of my official PCIs and you don't show anywhere in the Informant File, which is the way you damn sure want to keep it."

"I understand. I'll take nothing personal."

We paid the tab and went outside to our cars.

"Watch your step, Georgie. I hear things too. Take nothing or nobody for granted."

"Not even you, Danny-Boy?"

He chuckled. "Keep in touch."

It was the last time we talked before the roof caved in.

One day early in June a call came into the office and I immediately recognized the voice of a woman I had known for some time but never in the Biblical sense. But this was going too damned far; I couldn't be having these calls on the office phone. I slammed the receiver down and took off like I had good sense. I ran for my car and drove straight to her house — the biggest mistake of my life up until then.

She had barely opened the door when two vice detectives arrived and barged right in. I'd known one of them most of my life. "Sorry, George," he said, "orders." The woman said she was sorry too but had to cooperate or suffer the consequences.

They took me in and booked me for violations of a city ordnance against the uttering of harassing phone calls. The ordnance also covered lewd and lascivious calls, so take your pick. They even had a couple of recordings; my calls but none of the women's calls to me. They didn't bother to question me, and I had nothing to say in any case. I'd done enough talking.

I was out of the law firm overnight. But my mentor, William Earle Tucker, a senior partner in the firm and a former prosecutor, remained a comfort. The night of my dismissal he took me to a drive-in for burgers and fries. Then he drove down beside the river and parked. I broke down and told him everything, even some of my suspicions, but without the use of names. He was a friend to a friend in need. He told me to keep my mouth shut, to stay away from court and to have a *nolo* plea entered in my behalf. He arranged for my legal representation, and I did what he said. A *nolo contendere* plea was entered, meaning that I didn't admit or deny anything. I was convicted of a misdemeanor and fined all of $50.

A few days later I had coffee with the presiding judge. An old friend, he told me about the evidence offered at the hearing. One of the detectives said that I had paused on the target doorstep long enough to light and smoke a cigarette. I am now 76 years of age and have never smoked a cigarette in my life. The judge knew I was a non-smoker and so did everyone who had ever known me. "You must have really been hitting a raw nerve."

The phone rang a few nights later in the apartment. Pattie was with her mother, trying to hide her shame, and so I answered. The caller said: "Is this Paul Revere? Guess you'll keep your mouth shut from here on, hey."

It wasn't a question. It was a message that things could get a lot worse if I didn't hove to. And where the hell was *my* presidential protection unit? JFK had the Secret Service and a rich Daddy to clean up all his dirty messes. I was entirely on my own.

I'd never been so embarrassed and humiliated in my life. The kid, the Boy Scout, Mr. America was shown for what he really was, stripped bare and paraded before the public in all his shame. I, who had always considered myself so specially chosen and watched over, one who had always succeeded in whatever venture he might undertake, one to whom all things just seemed to come as entitlement now lay exposed and naked on the rack.

I ranted and raved in my misery, cursing myself, women in general, the covert scoundrels who had set all this up, and the ever-loving, all-seeing God who saw and ordained all.

In time, I got my life back in order. I moved into a new office set-up by way of advice from my old friend Al Cazin, who had introduced me to Pattie just before I went off for my military service. Al later engaged in a partnership with our buddies Paul Antinori, who had been a two-term state attorney, and Frank Ragano, who was an attorney for Santo, Marcello and Jimmy Hoffa and had been disbarred for such services. Al knew of a situation that was immediately available. Three lawyers shared office space in the Marine Bank Building downtown, a couple of blocks from the courthouse. One of the men had suddenly moved out and there was an empty office available. I agreed to terms at once and moved in. They agreed to share cases with me that they didn't normally handle themselves, mostly criminal and matrimonial cases. We would split fees, and I was free to develop my own practice accordingly. It was a fine arrangement, and I was soon making a fairly good living and loathing every moment of it.

I wished I could confer again with Fred Osborn, but that was impossible. I had neither seen nor heard from him since I left the Bureau. Danny McNight was now my primary Bureau confidant concerning serious matters of governmental importance. He told me about the collapse of Operation Mongoose and the covert CIA efforts to enlist the Mafia to murder Castro. And then, early in June, President Kennedy had delivered a speech at the American University in Washington, D.C. that resounded around the world.

This was a new Kennedy. There was no belligerence against other nations, no threats of American military might. Rather it was a plea for world peace and cooperative relations between previously committed adversaries. He encouraged all nations to work toward policies that sought to exploit the positive aspects of their differences. "If we cannot now end our differences," he said, "at least we can help make the world safe for diversity."

The entire world had been highly stressed by deepening fears of the radioactive fallout from the unregulated American and Soviet nuclear test programs, and the world took heart from the tone of the president's speech. Perhaps there was hope of a mutual détente between the U.S. and Soviet Union and therefore the prospect of world survival.

Even so, Danny was not optimistic. "There are disturbing currents and undercurrents racing about Miami," he told me.

Hit rumors were all over Miami regarding JFK's planned visit to Tampa on November 18. And such turmoil was certainly not limited to Miami. The Tampa-Ybor City underground was awash with seemingly fact-based information about assassination plans for the president's Tampa visit on that occasion. There was a veritable rogue's gallery of possible suspects: exiled hotheads, CIA covert elements, and top-level Mafiosi. Take your pick.

You may remember from the PROLOGUE that I'd already talked with my childhood friend, Boots Ruiz, and now I tried again to make contact with him but to no avail. He'd dropped entirely off the radar screen. I never saw him again. I actually wished I would hear from Martin and/or Adrian St. Cloud. I'd often obtained something useful from them, even if it was unintentional, but I had no way of contacting them and they were leaving me alone. Or had they been instrumental in my recent fall from grace? I never learned.

Nevertheless, I was able to piece together a pretty clear present-day picture from the uncoordinated information that I was accumulating from my friends, informants and confidants. What I saw was almost beyond rational belief.

The Mafia plot was to assassinate Kennedy in the Tampa motorcade on the 18th of this month. It would happen in downtown Tampa when the motorcade slowed almost to a stop on Florida Avenue in order to make a sharp left turn in front of the Floridian Hotel, the tallest building in town at that time. Professional hit men had been engaged to shoot the president using scoped high-powered rifles from a series of unprotected hotel windows. The hotel would be jammed with gawking tourists, and deep security would be almost impossible.

I had a longtime friend with the Tampa Police Department, an officer with a distinguished record, and he verified all of this for me, off the record of course.

And there was even a designated patsy already unknowingly set to take the fall. So far his identity was known only by the Secret Service presidential protection unit, but my friend said that they hadn't shared that information with local law enforcement. Naturally I couldn't help but wonder if *I* might be ... but then surely such thoughts were pure paranoid suspicion on my part.

My police friend suspected that whatever the patsy's identity, he was a planted CIA functionary on some sort of side mission with no idea of the imminent assassination plan involving the president. Tampa was already swarming with an advance party of Secret Service agents, he said, but he had no idea what they were doing. There appeared to be little that could effectively prevent an assassination attempt along the motorcade route.

What stunned me about this information was the certainty that the CIA was *not* involved in the assassination plot here in Tampa, that they were engaged in some other parallel but equally lethal mission that involved Mafia hired assassins. I assumed that it was the follow-up effort after the failure of Operation Mongoose to assassinate Fidel Castro.

A later conversation with Johnny Hicks added more uncertainty. "I have friends too, you know. What have you been told about the invasion preparations?"

"What invasion?" I asked and that surprised him.

"Better ask some of your sources."

I immediately called Danny, and he said, "Jesus! We can't discuss *this* on the phone. Tonight, you know where."

That night we met in St. Petersburg at a restaurant just across the bay. Danny had a beer and I my usual martini. He was highly agitated. "Who the hell you been talking to," he demanded at once, and I just shrugged. I certainly couldn't use Johnny's name or that of the police lieutenant. "Well, whoever it is, he better watch his mouth. And you better ..."

"C'mon, Danny. It's me, Georgie. Talk to me; don't just hang me out on a limb. What's this all about?"

I finally got him to loosen up a bit. It wasn't much, but maybe it was all that he knew. The planned Tampa hit was a Mafia operation entirely. They had another separate Castro hit operation going with the Company skunks, with the approval of both of the Kennedy brothers, but no CIA agents were overtly involved in *this* plan to assassinate the president here in Tampa. *This* was the work of Marcello, Trafficante and Johnny Roselli. Maybe some money was being furnished by Jimmy Hoffa, but the plan had nothing to do with Cuba and getting Castro as far as the mobsters were concerned. They just wanted to get rid of JFK in order to effectively quash Bobby's prosecutorial zeal.

But the plan *did* have something to do with Cuba, however, and this was the most crucial element of the entire operation. Cuba would make the mob's killing of Kennedy safe business, Danny had said, since the president's death would immediately inspire a blanket government cover-up.

"Cover up of what?" I had demanded.

It seems that all the Kennedy talk about appeasement with Castro was public eyewash. Mongoose was down, yes, but the CIA and Mafia still had an ongoing operation to assassinate Castro underway, an operation that did not involve the Kennedy brothers. They had not even been told of it.

But now for the shocker: the Kennedys had a covert *military* mission of their own underway to promote a coup in Cuba to be followed by a U.S. *military* invasion! And incredibly, all this was to be accomplished with CIA participation, although the Agency would have nothing to do with the planning and no decision-making power.

The plan was crafted and then organized under the highest level security, higher even than Top Secret. Besides the Chairman of the Joint Chiefs of Staff, General Maxwell Taylor, only one or two of the other Chiefs were aware of the Cuba planning. Even the military men in intensive training maneuvers at various posts had no idea what they were preparing for. And probably no more than half a dozen officials in the Kennedy administration had any notion of what was going on.

Danny didn't know the name of the operation, few people did, and it was quite some time before I learned that it had been code-named "C-Day" and that an invasion date had even been set: December 1, 1963! The plan had Jack's full support and Bobby was in operational control.

But it stretched credulity to think that the mob had not infiltrated the planning of C-Day. After all, mobster Johnny Roselli was a longtime Company asset, as was Santo. Therefore, the mob had to know all about C-Day, and the Company in turn had to know about the Mafia plot to assassinate JFK.

In any case, the invasion aspect of the Tampa assassination plan would have to be concealed at all costs. So if the Mafia did manage to kill JFK in Tampa, their role could not be pinned on them and risk exposing the Cuban military invasion plan and the attendant assassination of Castro. The mob saw it as a foolproof operation. Because the public knew that the government had long been aware of previous CIA/Mafia attempts to kill Castro, the murder of Kennedy would not be placed on the Mafia's doorstep. Castro, in fact, could even be blamed for the deed.

This subterfuge required a patsy to be immediately eliminated and followed by an intense cover-up blitz after the dirty deed was accomplished.

I had coffee on the morning of the 16th with my friend, the police lieutenant with TPD. "The patsy's identity is known, Georgie." He grinned and said, "Breathe easy, it's not you. He's a local boy, Cuban, an ex-Marine and a Castro supporter, said to be linked to that Oswald guy over in New Orleans in their Fair Play for Cuba shenanigans. And, like Oswald, he's a former defector with Russian connections. No, don't ask, I won't tell you his name."

"Why don't you just pick him up on a pretext violation and keep him out of circulation?"

He shifted uneasily and his face colored with a rush of anger. "Actually, I don't personally know his name, so the P.D. can't pick him up. The fucking Secret Service won't tell us his name! Talk around headquarters is that he's also a government asset, for what agency I don't know, so his identity has to be protected until he's needed."

"Needed to be killed, you mean?"

But what the hell was *I* going to do? None of this concerned me in any official way, so why not just go to my office and attend to the business at hand. In a pig's eye. I *couldn't* let it go. I called my only source in the Tampa FBI field office.

I will use the name Bob Royce (nowhere near the true name of my contact) for convenience and safety. We had been friends from the first day of my enlistment, before my acceptance actually. I liked him and respected him. Like Danny, he was highly exercised over what I knew about all of this and how I had obtained the information. I finally calmed him down and we began to talk.

"Tampa is the second piece of the operation," he said. "They were going to nail him in Chicago back on November 2, but JFK suddenly cancelled his visit. I don't know the details. Nothing official and nothing has been publicly released. But there's plenty of talk. Motorcade through the city, president in an open vehicle, snipers using high-powered rifles from tall buildings, and a Fair Play for Cuba patsy set up to take the fall." If Bob knew about C-Day he said nothing about that aspect of the hit plan.

"And now the mob has learned from their mistakes, ironed out the wrinkles," I suggested, "and will finish the job here in Tampa."

Time was so damned short. President Kennedy would be in Tampa on the 18th and the shit would hit the fan.

The day dawned warm and bright; a perfect day for a parade. Pattie and I had an early breakfast, and then she left for work. I had long since rearranged all of my cases and office appointments. I'd had the TV on all morning but there was nothing except the excitement of the pending presidential visit. No alarm bells, no warnings. What could *I* do? I had already anonymously called every source I could think of, state, federal and local.

But the day passed without incident. I stood just a few feet from the passing vehicles, spoke to the president, wished him good luck; he waved in return, and then the limousine passed on to its next destination.

No shots were fired in Tampa. President John F. Kennedy's rendezvous with death was in another city.

Censored

The photograph that belongs here shows JFK on the autopsy table with his head back, eyes open and looking heavenward. His mouth is open too — what might he have wanted to tell us? The visible entrance wound in his throat is clear evidence that the shot that caused the wound came from the front — the grassy knoll? — and that Oswald or anyone else could not have acted alone, firing all the shots that hit the president from the Texas Book Depository to the rear of the presidential motorcade. This one photograph — and there are many others — is proof that the Warren Commission lied. And the conspiracy continues to this day in the most important unsolved murder case in American history:

Permission to use the autopsy photograph in this book was denied on pain of civil suit and/or prosecution. However, the autopsy photographs do exist, and can be found on the Internet.

PART TEN

Appointment in Dallas

On November 22, 1963, I was eating lunch alone in the apartment. Pattie was at work and I'd shut down my office operations. My television had been on all morning. Jack and Jackie, were in Ft. Worth preparing for the final push into Dallas. The president would make a breakfast speech and then would depart via Air Force One.

On this morning, Jack was said to have announced to his staff that it would be a great day for an assassination. He said it would be easy for a sniper to shoot him from a hi-rise window with a scoped automatic rifle. This kind of talk was nothing new for the fatalistic president, and no one was really shocked. He had lived with near death for so long that he was hardened to such talk and morbid thoughts. I have often wondered if he had received word of the pending assassination plans in Chicago, Tampa and Dallas, which would have accounted for such morbidity. But wouldn't he have done *something* had he possessed such detailed warnings? I had the morning newspaper spread across the table, having searched in vain again for any mention of the failed assassination plot here in Tampa on the 18th. There was not a word, nor would there be such comment until after the successful assassination in Dallas, and then there would only be one local article never to be repeated.

The news media nationwide was equally mute. Not a word in any Texas media outlet, including Dallas, concerning recent presidential assassination plots in Chicago and Tampa. The Secret Service continued to operate in a realm of deep secrecy indeed. And just how much did *they* know? Never mind the fact that it was their job to know.

The FBI was good at playing its cards close to the vest, too. Consider this bit of information that came to me in a follow-up talk with Bob Royce. After JFK had safely departed Tampa, Bob had told me about the FBI teletype warning from Director Hoover to all Bureau offices on the 17th. The warning read as follows:

URGENT: 1:45 a.m. EST 11-17-63 HLF 1 PAGE
TO: ALL SACS
FROM: DIRECTOR

THREAT TO ASSASSINATE PRESIDENT KENNEDY IN DALLAS TEXAS NOVEMBER 22 DASH TWENTY THREE NINETEEN SIXTY THREE.

MISC INFORMATION CONCERNING. INFORMATION HAS BEEN RECEIVED BY THE BUREAS (sic) BUREAU HAS DETERMINED THAT A MILITANT REVOLUTIONARY GROUP MAY ATTEMPT TO ASSASSINATE PRESIDENT KENNEDY ON HIS PROPOSED TRIP TO DALLAS TEXAS NOVEMBER TWENTY TWO DASH TWENTY THREE NINETEEN SIXTY THREE.

ALL RECEIVING OFFICES SHOULD IMMEDIATELY CONTACT ALL CIS, PCI LOGICAL RACE AND HATE GROUP INFORMANTS AND DETERMINE IF ANY BASIS FOR THREAT.

BUREAU SHOULD BE KEPT ADVISED OF ALL DEVELOPMENTS BY TELETYPE.

OTHER OFFICES HAVE BEEN ADVISED.

END AND ACK PLS.

A few agents around the country made copies of the teletype, which was a good thing since immediately after the assassination the message disappeared from all Bureau offices nationwide.

"And the worst part of all of this," Bob had said, "is the fact that, in spite of all legal requirements to the contrary, the Old Man refused to notify any other agencies of the threat, including Secret Service, CIA and military intelligence sources."

And here we have a perfect example of one of the greatest weaknesses of governmental operations: the unwillingness of one agency to trust its information in the hands of a sister agency. "Turf protection," field workers call it. Of course, no agency would share such important data with members of the media.

I can feel it as I write, so many of you jumping ahead in time to the dark days of 9/11/01.

On that fateful Friday in 1963, my telephone rang at 12:30 p.m. and continued ringing as I sat glued to the TV. Walter Cronkite had already told us that the president had been shot and now, at 1 PM, he told the world in a breaking voice that President Kennedy was dead.

By three o'clock that afternoon I found myself down by the riverside alone and dazed. I didn't want to see anyone, didn't want to talk with anyone. I didn't know how I got there, or what I was doing or wanted to do or was going to do. Jack was dead, most of his head blown off. I don't know when I'd started to cry. Then I was in the car again and it was moving.

That evening I found myself in the apartment. Pattie was there, her eyes red and swollen. She said that all of my friends were looking for me. The phone kept ringing. She would answer and hold the receiver out to me but I took no calls. I simply sat staring at the TV. Finally Pattie said, "I think you need to take this one."

She put the phone to my ear and I mumbled, "What?"

"Get on your horse and ride fast." I won't say the name of the caller but I knew the voice and knew I had to respond. The instructions had been clear and concise. "Go to the Holiday Inn, ease into the restaurant, but stay in back undetected."

Our apartment was but minutes away from the hotel. I passed through the same lobby in which JFK had recently stood shaking hands toward the end of his Tampa visit. I eased discretely into the restaurant and took a seat in back near a potted palm. Few tables were occupied; most potential diners were glued to their televisions. But I knew exactly why I had been sent here. At a table near the front sat Santo Trafficante and his attorney, Frank Ragano. They were drinking and laughing and Santo signaled their waiter for more champagne.

I shoved back in my chair and covered my face as Frank's girlfriend and future wife brushed past me on her way to the table. Santo stood and held her chair and then signaled for another glass. They talked together for a few moments and when the glasses were filled Santo raised his in a toasting gesture and Frank joined him. I was too far away to hear what was said but it was obviously a buoyant toast to the propitious passing of John F. Kennedy.

Frank's girl leaped to her feet, tossed her napkin on the table and bolted from the room. Santo and Frank watched her go and then the toasting recommenced. At their table jubilation reigned.

I got out of there fast and soon learned that Santo and Frank's was not the only celebratory eruption following the president's death. In New Orleans, almost at the precise time of JFK's fatal wounding in Dallas, the trial of Carlos Marcello on a charge of conspiracy to defraud and obstruct the United States government in the exercise of its right to deport him was winding down.

At the same time, Attorney General Robert F. Kennedy, who had spearheaded the prosecution of the New Orleans don, was meeting with his organized crime team in D.C. to formulate new attack plans against the leading organized crime figures in America, focusing on Mafia chiefs Carlos Marcello, Santo Trafficante, Sam Giancana and labor outcast Jimmy Hoffa. At 2:15 Washington time, however, a phone call from J. Edgar Hoover interrupted Bobby's lunch with the one-sentence news that his brother had been shot. Robert Kennedy's special unit investigating organized crime in America would never meet again.

Meanwhile back in New Orleans, the closing arguments and judicial charge to the jury had just concluded when a court bailiff entered the courtroom and passed the judge a note. He read the note and rose in visible shock to make the announcement that the president had been shot in Dallas and was presumed dead.

At 3:15 New Orleans time the foreman of the trial jury read the verdict: Not guilty on all charges.

Marcello embraced his attorneys, hugged and kissed his family and friends, and strode from the courtroom in triumph. Now his only worry was whether all events had gone as planned in Dallas. And with the planned murder of Lee Harvey Oswald by mob henchman Jack Ruby, most of the deed would be over and done. All that would remain was the elimination of Ruby, and that would come soon enough.

Ruby Murders Oswald

In Washington D.C., J. Edgar Hoover and Clyde had supper and then went home to watch the continuing coverage of the assassination on television. The next day they went to the races. At nearby Pimlico, they assumed their regular free-gratis seats and enjoyed drinks and finger food, placed their bets, lost every race and never paid a cent.

The remaining items on the cleanup detail were left to President Johnson's sacrosanct Warren Commission, including the final cover-up of the truth concerning the assassination of the President of the United States.

I don't remember sleeping or eating for days after the news of the 22nd and the shocking performance of my two former friends at the Holiday Inn late that night.

Death, the end of all life; death, the only certainty in life. Shall we wait for it? Or go out and seek it? Perhaps *that* is our only answer; that we should each go forth in search of our own appointments in Dallas and any other venue that awaits our final arrival.

The world changed in 1963 with JFK's bloody assassination. I, along with millions, was devastated. It was the worst trauma I had experienced in my active life to date. And then in June of 1968, we suffered the murder of Bobby when it became apparent that he would soon become the next president of the United States.

Lyndon Baines Johnson

PART ELEVEN

Days of Lies and Deceptions

Is there any one fact that is today unassailable concerning the assassination of John F. Kennedy and the official report of how the terrible act occurred and who was responsible for his death? I suggest that the answer is a resounding, *Yes!*

The government lied to us then and persists in the lie and cover-up even today concerning the most important unsolved murder case in American history.

Most of us know the official story-line put forth by the President's Commission on the Assassination of President Kennedy, created by Executive Order of President Lyndon B. Johnson on November 29, 1963. On that fateful day in Dallas, November 22, 1963, according to Commission conclusions, President Kennedy was killed by three shots fired from a window of the Texas School Book Depository; three rounds fired from a mail-order Mannlicher-Carcano rifle with a telescopic site; the shooter being a left-wing misfit named Lee Harvey Oswald who was acting on his own warped initiative.

The Committee presented their deceitful conclusion to President Johnson on September 24, 1964. The conclusion was verbatim with the conclusion announced back on November 22, 1963 by city, state and federal authorities within approximately thirty minutes of the shooting. Gunshot residue still wafted on the air over Dealey Plaza when the name and a detailed description of the assailant were on the airwaves.

Allen W. Dulles

How could the Commission's conclusion be in such complete consistence with the original speculations on the date of

219

the crime? Was nothing useful learned in all of that time?

The members of the Commission were leading citizens of our day. But would the public today be surprised to learn that the Commission as a whole rarely met together in counsel and deliberation, and that the only member to have attended all sessions of the proceedings was Allen W. Dulles? He was the former Director of the CIA who had been fired by President Kennedy for incompetence and deception after the disastrous 1961 Bay of Pigs invasion of Cuba. The invasion had been sponsored by Dulles; his brother John Foster Dulles, former Secretary of State; and Richard M. Nixon, who had served as the White House action officer for the invasion created by then President Dwight D. Eisenhower.

Wasn't the Warren Commission capable of learning anything helpful in the course of its bogus deliberations? The only evidence presented to the Commission for deliberation was that supplied by J. Edgar Hoover and the FBI. Of course, Hoover had already publicly announced on the day of the assassination that Lee Harvey Oswald was the sole shooter of the president and that no accomplices were involved.

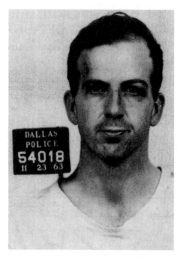

Lee Harvey Oswald

Might it have been of interest to the Commission had Hoover's intrepid investigators revealed covert evidence regarding the pre-arranged C-Day invasion of Cuba scheduled for December 1, 1963, along with knowledge of the contemporaneous assassination plans to kill Kennedy first in Chicago and then in Tampa, all as previously discussed herein in earlier chapters? Not one word of this was presented to the Commission.

And what if the Commission had been told that at least three of the designated patsies for the Chicago and Tampa plot were in Dallas on the 22nd? Might such information have led the Commission to debate possible motives and participation of other conspirators besides Lee Harvey Oswald? As in Chicago and

Tampa, might Oswald have been just what he said he was publicly after his arrest: a patsy?

I suggest that Commission members should have been interested to have learned that most of the Secret Service agents assigned to protect the president were hung over in varying degrees on the 22nd as a result of all-night binges in clubs controlled by Jack Ruby, lifelong associate of top-ranking mobsters in Chicago and Los Angeles, New Orleans, Tampa and Havana; experienced purveyor of drugs; world-wide gunrunner par excellence; and mob bag man to important law enforcement and judicial figures.

Certainly questions might have been asked as to why there were no Secret Service agents on the ground in Dallas on the morning of the 22nd, especially in the vicinity of the grassy knoll, an obvious shooting vantage point that posed a particular threat to the president. Also there might have been questions asked about why the customary military Presidential Protection Unit had been ordered to stand down that morning, and who gave such an order and why? But the Commission had none of this information, and no such queries were made.

And had the Commission met in joint session on a regular basis, isn't it fair to assume that someone would have inquired about why there was no gun residue on Oswald's hands or clothing immediately after his arrest as was verified by FBI laboratory specialists along with FBI findings that there were no Oswald prints on the alleged murder weapon that day?

And what of the fact that Oswald was confronted by building officials and a Dallas police detective within minutes following the shooting while he was in the second floor lunchroom of the Book Depository building? How could he have been on the sixth floor in order to commit the shooting, clean up the shooter's nest, conceal the rifle on the other side of the sixth floor and get downstairs in time to be confronted in the lunchroom?

Would anyone have asked detailed questions about why the initial televised description of the murder weapon by Dallas law enforcement officers and the Dallas District Attorney was that of a 7.65 mm German Mauser rather than a Mannlicher-Carcano, according the final and official description?

Hoover's mandate to gather evidence and present it to the Commission was in furtherance of the orders of his close friend and long-time covert conspirator President Johnson. And this was pursuant to one of the worst kept secrets in Washington D.C. Both men, Hoover and Johnson, detested the Kennedy brothers and were delighted to see the end of Kennedy influence on government affairs.

This is a memoir, a product of my recollection of known and acquired information regarding events of that day. I possessed a great deal from first-hand life experience, and as time passed I assiduously researched other events. Nevertheless, this is not an academic history but entirely an account of recovered memory and my continuing effort to learn more about those times and momentous events. My life has never been the same since that time.

These are the facts concerning the murder of President Kennedy.

The assassination of the president did not occur in the manner that has been force-fed to the American public by our government for nearly half a century. Today a vast majority of the American public intelligently disbelieves the published report of the Warren Commission.

More than three shots were fired that day and from various directions. We know that one shot missed Kennedy and the presidential limousine entirely, wounding a nearby civilian observer.

Shortly before the assassination, eyewitnesses behind the fence on the grassy knoll saw Jack Ruby drop off a passenger who was carrying a wrapped rifle and assumed a position behind the fence.

Countless witnesses claimed to have seen and heard shots fired from behind the fence on the grassy knoll. There were no Secret Service agents assigned to this area who could have witnessed all of this suspicious activity.

Abraham Zapruder filmed the last fatal moments of the assassination, a film that graphically shows how and when the president was shot.

But the members of the Warren Commission were never shown the Zapruder film! The graphic information on the film was not presented by the FBI as evidence. And even the public at large did not see the film until after a delay of five years.

As previously stated, Oswald was *not* on the sixth floor of the Texas Book Depository at the time of the shooting; Jack Ruby was witnessed before and after the shooting of the president; emergency room doctors at Parkland Memorial Hospital all agreed that the wound in Kennedy's throat was an entrance wound and that the fatal head shot, the hole in the back of his head, was an exit wound. The evidence indicates that neither Oswald nor anyone else killed Kennedy alone, that there were more than three shots, that there had to have been more than one shooter and that the shots came from more than one direction. There were no magic bullets that zigzagged this way and that and wounded both Kennedy and Governor John Connally who was riding in the limousine jump seat just in front of the president's position.

The Warren Commission, President Johnson, the Secret Service, Hoover and the FBI lied about the assassination.

Now a few random facts to consider:

On the night of November 21 extending into the early morning hours, another rogue's gallery had gathered in Dallas. A cocktail function for invited guests was held at the secure mansion of oilman Clint Murchison. In attendance were Vice President Lyndon B. Johnson, FBI Director J. Edgar Hoover, and former Vice President Richard M. Nixon. The discussion among the men was not recorded or, if a record was made of the imminent expectations of these men, none has ever surfaced.

Murchison and Hoover were long time friends, dare I say conspirators. The wealthy Murchison owned hotels and race tracks in which Hoover was a cherished guest throughout the years at no cost to the director. He maintained similar relations with Nixon and Johnson and many other government officials, all of whom had proved to be advantageous friends over the years.

In the early hours of the 22nd, Hoover flew back to Washington HQ by private plane, and shortly thereafter Richard Nixon flew commercially to his business office in New York City. Upon later questioning, Nixon first said that he couldn't remember where he was on November 22, 1963! Upon further consideration, however, he remembered that he was indeed in Dallas to attend a non-existent Board of Directors meeting of the Pepsi-Cola Company, of which he was a director. And evidence later given by the mistress of LBJ, and the mother of his illegitimate child, was that he had returned to her boudoir in the early morning hours of the 22nd and boasted that the damned Kennedy brothers would never humiliate him again!

And it might be of interest to the public, though not to the Warren commissioners, that the Texas Book Depository building was owned by Clint Murchison.

Had you been a member of the Committee might you have been curious as to why the vast majority of eye witnesses to the assassination all testified that they had seen and heard numerous shots and smoke release from behind the fence on the grassy knoll, testimony verified by members of the Kennedy staff such as Kenneth O'Donnell and David Powers who were riding in the car directly behind the presidential limousine?

Would you have asked how police could have observed Oswald in the second floor lunchroom of the Book Depository scant minutes after the president was shot and still have been on the sixth floor having fired those shots? Would you have asked what it meant that FBI lab tests established as a fact that in the absence of paraffin residue on his hands and clothing that Oswald could *not* have fired a gun of any make that day?

And what of the established fact that on the day of the assassination FBI tests revealed that Oswald's prints were *not* on the alleged murder weapon although some time after his residence in the county morgue new tests revealed his palm prints on the stock of the previously clean murder weapon? Would you have suspected that police officials had imposed his prints on the rifle stock?

After Oswald's arrest and interrogation at the Dallas police station no written or recorded account of his words was made. One of Oswald's questioners in the interrogation room was Texan George H. W. Bush, soon to become Director of CIA and a future president of the United States.

The official autopsy was conducted in Washington after President Kennedy's body had been illegally removed by federal authorities from the Dallas local officials who had rightly taken possession of the body. In that day there was no special federal law that made the shooting of the president a federal crime as there is today. The assassination of President John F. Kennedy was an offense against the laws of the state of Texas, and as such, the crime and all evidence pertaining to it should have remained in the custody of state officials. A trial to determine the identity of the shooters and the circumstances of the crime should have been litigated in a state court with official jurisdiction of the crime. JFK's body and all crucial evidence of the shooting, however, were removed under protest from Parkland Hospital in Dallas by armed federal officials.

The subsequent autopsy took place at Bethesda Naval Hospital in Washington D.C. The autopsy from first to last was a flawed farce. Inexperienced doctors who were totally unfamiliar with criminal autopsies performed the surgery. These doctors, however, did and later said what they were instructed to say and do. The military attendants supervised the entire medical procedure under the control of Robert F. Kennedy.

Bobby was the driving force behind the removal of the body from Dallas and the autopsy procedure at Bethesda. He was in the surgical room much of the time and when elsewhere in the building his representatives remained behind hovering over the autopsy table. Bobby interfered to safeguard any word concerning the super-secret C-Day plans. The illegal invasion plan had to be concealed at all costs.

Autopsy results had to support the official theory of Oswald as the single shooter of the president. Therefore, his back wound had to be raised to a lower neck wound to substantiate the "Magic bullet" theory, and the small entrance wound in his throat had to be enlarged to resemble an exit wound. The massive exit wound in the back of the head presented the major problem. No matter what was said in the final autopsy report, a later examination of the president's brain would have revealed the wound to have been the result of a massive exit wound from a frontal shot. Conspiracy! This could not be allowed. So, the brain must be lost!

To this day there is no brain to attest to the direction of the fatal shot, which of course would reveal a conspiracy, the existence of which would lead to questions about the nature of such a conspiracy and ultimately C-Day would be exposed. And this Bobby and those involved could not allow. They still hoped that the public would finally place the blame for the president's murder on Fidel Castro, and an invasion of Cuba would be demanded with full justification.

To quote Sir Walter Scott: *"Oh what tangled webs we weave, When first we practice to deceive."*

John Fitzgerald Kennedy

PART TWELVE

Epilogue

After the assassination and following an extended period of grief and alcoholic self-abuse, I came to realize that a sane, constructive way of life was still possible for me. I, among so many others, had been unable to prevent the assassination and save President Kennedy's life, but there was still a chance to save myself. At least, I had to try.

My efforts, however, were not without obstacles. Martin was once again on my scent. We met beside the river with the spires of Tampa University in sight on the other side. He looked about the same, a little more worn and washed out. "Can we finally talk? Surely you can see what dangers there are in this world. Why wouldn't you want to be on the side of the strong rather than take your chances with the disorganized marauders?"

"Is this why you invited me down here? More of the same old same old? Why won't you just leave me alone?"

"I *won't* leave you alone, so sit."

"I don't want to sit with you, *Marteen,* or any of your filthy kind."

I had turned and started back up the grassy slope when he called out. "Well watch your back, kid! If we can reach presidents, we can damn sure ..."

But that was as far as he got. I whirled and ran back down the grassy slope, grabbed him by the collar of his suit coat with one hand and clutched the seat of his pants with the other. He was twisting and pulling, and his hat fell off, but he couldn't break loose from my grasp. He began to bellow when he realized what was going to happen.

I manhandled him for three or four more steps, grunted, and then heaved him over the railing with all my accumulated fury. He was waving his arms and legs as he plunged into the water. I turned and started back up the hillside.

"You'll be sorry for this!" he screamed with his arms flapping as he struggled to get his head above water. "Do you hear me? I'll make you so sorry ..."

But I got in my car. I started the engine and said out loud, "I'm already sorry. I'm so fucking sorry that words can't describe my pain."

I shifted into future gear and drove away as his head emerged above the railing.

****

I will move ahead now in order to tie up loose ends and to preview the future. Pattie and I moved to Grand Cayman early in 1965. We lived in West Bay in a lovely island cottage with her Aunt Stella.

I was the co-owner and editor of the island weekly newspaper, The Tradewinds. As such, I had access to all the nooks and crannies of island life. I became friends with the British Administrator (Governor in today's parlance) and was a regular invited guest at Government House. I met judges, Crown prosecutors, barristers and businessmen of stature and influence. And I met Calypso singers, bargirls, and countless ladies of the night.

You can imagine how much I loved all of this, the people with whom I worked, those I met in the course of my duties and social affairs, and the exotic Cayman way of life. All of which offered so much raw material to write about. I began and completed my first novel while working under the Cayman sun.

One night Pattie and I attended a private soirée at Government House located on Seven Mile Beach, property once owned by her family. There were lots of food and drink and much conviviality. Pattie was dancing, and as I accepted another glass of wine from the steward, I saw him: Adrian St. Cloud, standing across the room, tall, erect and dapper in Panama whites with a drink in one hand and his ever present onyx cigarette holder in the other. Our eyes locked and he smiled through his horn rims and started my way. "I say, dear boy, how good t'see you again."

As smarmy as ever and I laughed as we shook hands. "I heard about the confrontation on the riverside in Tampa. Always been something of an ass, a dip in the briny might have done him some good."

"So why are you here, cruising for a dip in the sea?"

He laughed and we moved over beside a large window that opened on the pristine beach below. The calypso music in the background masked our conversation.

"Pushed for time, so I'll get right to the point. You can now be of even greater service to your country. This position with the press, do y'see; your cover now is perfect. And after Cayman, you can go anywhere you choose, dragging a somewhat blemished reputation as you set forth to see the world and to write a string of raunchy novels."

He lit another cigarette and repeated, "It's a perfect cover, and we'll run you through our Tourist Department." He saw the look of consternation on my face. "Nobody's heard of it: includes writers, artists, movie makers, even school teachers. Now you've heard of it, but you will never mention it. Just be ready when ..."

My anger boiled over. "Don't you get it, don't any of you rogue elephants get it! I'm through with you guys. I ..."

"Come along, George." He hooked my arm and said, "A stroll on the beach and a bit of fresh air will set things right."

We walked down through the garden out to the beach. The powder-white sand was glowing in the moonlight, and it seemed that you might be able to walk the moon path across the water right up into the velvet heavens.

"Have you the slightest notion what the potential is for creative intrigue down here in the Caribbean basin? Of course you must have. Off-shore banking capabilities here in Grand Cayman are just in their infancy. I figure your 'family' friends have already sounded you out." A few had done so but I'd not listened to them either, and I certainly wasn't going to drop any names to St. Cloud.

"And Cuba is just beyond eyesight. El *gran lider* is still there, George, and we still want him out." There was no mention of C-Day that might still be waiting in the wings. "And all of this is where you come in, laddie."

Now I exploded. This was just too damn much. I couldn't go into this dark night again without effective protest. I whirled on him with all the pent up anger, guilt, fear and regret that had been lodged in my throat for so long that I was apt to choke on it if I couldn't get it out.

"If I had a gun I really think I would kill you, Adrian, for the good of our country and the world. Because you can't help it; you'll never change. You're a sick man, brain and soul gone to rot; you and all the rest of your perverted bunch. And what's worse is that you lunatics *know* it and still you enjoy what you are doing.

"It's the sense of power over other people's lives, isn't it, over whole nations. Just how many bad guys are on your shit list besides Castro in this on-going stand-up-for-Jesus and Democracy crusade? Indochina still raging, Africa next, and then the entire heathen Middle East? Where will it end? Do you guys even visualize an ending?"

I was becoming totally unglued. "What is it you dorks call yourselves — the *intelligence community*? Jesus, what an oxymoron! The whole process is out of control. You bastards don't have any idea who you are. You're no better than the bad guys; hell, you're just like them. Change the uniform, wave a different flag, yawp a variation of some sacred ism and you're all the fucking same: communists, fascists, mobsters, government deviants. And you deceitful tricksters know it; you know you have no cause worth fighting and dying for, so you let others fight and die while you live only for the game. Gamesters, that's what you clowns are."

I ran to the beach, and Adrian followed until I whirled around and faced him with clenched fists. "Kennedy understood, at least he was learning, and maybe that's why he had to be killed. I know all about his flaws, he wasn't perfect by a long shot; but he was trying to get a grip on things, trying to stuff all the mad genies back into the bottle.

"And that's it, isn't it? *That's* why he was killed. It wasn't poor, pitiful Lee Oswald, I know that and *you* know that. It wasn't a handful of exile fanatics, Mafiosi, or a gang of right-wing Super Patriots operating on their own. No, John Kennedy was a threat to all the power brokers, corporate and government, the warmongers, the briefcase gangsters and their easy-money cronies. Yeah, the ones who really call the shots, right? John and Bobby were zeroing in, and the goons were scared to death, right?"

Adrian flicked ashes from his cigarette and finally spoke up. "You are playing with fire again, Georgie, touching on things …"

"And Bobby knows all of this too, so is *he* next?"

"Stop it!" he said. "Stop this right now before …"

I grabbed him by his shoulders and shook him so hard that his false teeth rattled.

"Goddamn it, Adrian, don't you understand? *We killed him!* You, me, the Company, Hoover, the Mafia, the industrialists and the oil barons — all of us, we're all to blame. It was the times, we wallowed in deceit and deception, and our country has paid the price — is still paying today — the price of our corruption. But it isn't just business as usual now, not anymore, not now. It's different. Can't you *see* that?"

I bolted into the sea, hoping for the arrival of a Caribbean tsunami. Adrian came no further than the water's edge.

"People in our country will never be the same," I called above the sloughing wave sound. "The government will never be the same. To be an American will never mean the same thing ever again. You guys, me, all of us ... we killed more than a man, more than a president." My eyes filled with tears and I could hardly see him. "We killed an idea — the idea of what we are and of what we might have become. And it's gone now, possibly forever gone."

As I came out of the sea Adrian removed his onyx flask from his coat pocket.

"I say, dear boy. You'd best join me in a good stiff head knocker, what?"

****

Things did not go well between Pattie and me. We both made mistakes which we were unable to patch over. And after some three years in our island in the sun, we decided to return to Tampa where each would go the way of choice. We remained friends, but Pattie moved in with her mother, and I went off to Mexico with my Loyola friend and confidant, Father Bernard Tonnar, S.J.

Now some of you may ask what all of this has to do with the assassination of President Kennedy. I think it is important to show how events of the past impact those of the future. Kennedy was dead but most of the players in that atrocity were still at large and actively operational.

Bernie was now Dean of Students at Loyola and Director of International Studies at the National University in Mexico City. He seemed to know everyone of high and low social standing and was friends to all. He also seemed to be involved in some covert government business — what branch I never knew for certain — but it was clear to me that he had his finger on the pulse of boiling events in that great but troubled city.

Phil Agee was by then an experienced Company officer assigned to the station in Mexico City. He told me over breakfast one morning that Adrian St. Cloud was also in and out of the city, but I didn't cross paths with him in this interval of time. Gratefully, Martin continued to cut me a wide swath.

My sojourn in Mexico City was brought to a sudden halt by an outbreak of revolutionary zeal centered on the University campus. Agee contacted me late one night and warned me to avoid the Zocalo Plaza the next morning, and St. Cloud left a note in my hotel message box advising me that I should leave for home immediately. So, with all these alarm bells ringing from people in the know, what did I do? I rushed down to the Plaza that morning and watched as the roiling crowd began to swell by the tens of thousands.

I detected the rumble of the approaching tanks and personnel carriers and I withdrew to a doorway on the outer perimeter of the Plaza. The troops opened fire on the panic-stricken targets with machine guns and automatic weapons. The helpless victims made up a conglomeration of tens of thousands of men, women, children and young student revolutionaries who had not fired a shot or lobbed a single Molotov cocktail in the course of their exuberant demands for change and justice.

The U.S. news media along with the rest of the world accepted and reissued the Mexican government's official report of the unfortunate injuries that occurred as a result of the behavior of a mob of out of control revolutionaries. The report acknowledged the injuries of ten or twelve agitators and the unfortunate deaths of two or three. The true count, however, was in the thousands.

Back home beneath the shady pines of my Georgia farmstead, I wrote about the government atrocity I'd witnessed in Mexico City in my second attempt at a novel. My first effort, the island novel, had earned no offers to publish. The first book had taken almost three years to write, while this second effort was completed in five weeks of intensive labor.

I had it typed and in the mail while still trying to absorb all that I had seen and learned from my adventure in Mexico and how it might influence my future plans.

But I left for Tampa without even the outline of a future life plan, unaware that soon I would be living in a world of best sellerdom. My world had already changed in 1963 with JFK's bloody assassination, and I along with millions was devastated.

Darlene Mettler

And then in June of 1968, the murder of Bobby Kennedy further devastated my sensibilities and those of the American public.

And still more change was soon to come my way. I had no way of knowing that I was about to encounter a glorious change in my life that would absorb my loving attention for the next forty years: Darlene.

And that's the way it was for me in an earlier time, a time that is still with us in so many ways.

Now the end of March, 2011 finds me once again in my secluded cabin in the Georgia pines and stationed at my writing desk. In the three year interval since I began work on this memoir I have traveled with it to London, Oxford, Paris and Provence, and soon I will depart for an extended sojourn in Spain.

I would have visited Agee in Havana, the only place in the world that would harbor him from CIA vengeance for the tell-all book that he'd published about his years with the Agency. We had maintained contact through mutual friends and he'd offered to help with my literary labors any way that he could. But due to my wife Darlene's illness I was unable to make the trip and now that I am free to travel I find that Agee has kept another appointment with a higher authority. So my present tale ends here.

But I can stop with clear heart and conscience for I have kept my promise to Darlene. Remember, as she closed her eyes she made me promise to tell my story. And here it is.

I have since taken her ashes back to her beloved London where the waters of the Thames have lovingly washed her to her final resting place. I will tell you about this remarkable woman in a subsequent book; my lover, wife and boon companion, the mother of my two sons and my everlasting soul mate. Yes, I will tell you about her so that you will know just what kind of special spirit has walked among us.

I promise.

George Mettler Self Portrait

About the Author

George B. Mettler is a published author of seven novels and one book of nonfiction, a text book on criminal investigation. His major interests dating from his boyhood include a desire to be in the FBI, to write books and to paint. To say the least, his career is eclectic. He has been a successful high school and college athlete, an Army officer engaged in undercover counter intelligence work in Mexico, an FBI agent during the Kennedy administration, and a practicing attorney of civil and criminal law, much of it with an international flavor. In addition, Mettler has co-owned two weekly newspapers and served as a financial advisor in this country and abroad.

His career choices have caused him to live and work in many parts of the world, including Mexico, the Caribbean, Europe and North Africa. In addition to his residence in Georgia, he has had homes in Grand Cayman, London and Malaga/Marbella, Spain. He also speaks Spanish and Japanese. His first novel, published in 1970, sold more than one million copies. His successive works probably have sold a total of more than one million. His output, however, tapered off drastically in the late 1900s and worsened after 2000 when his late wife, a successful and well-known academician, was diagnosed with incurable cancer, stage four. Ultimately, she was given six months to live. She waged her battle for six years! During the final six or eight months of her life, she was a near-paraplegic, requiring Mettler's full-time attention. In March, 2008, his wife passed away.

Secrets and Lies: Memoir of the Kennedy Years is based on Mettler's experience as an FBI agent, along with his personal relationships with such notorious characters as godfathers Santo Trafficante and Carlos Marcello; CIA renegade agent Philip Agee; Lee Harvey Oswald and his family; Guy Banister; Clay Shaw; David Ferrie; Jack Ruby and others. This book will

Mettler in Spain, 2001

shred the bogus Warren Report on the assassination, with little or nothing held back, and should ignite a firestorm of renewed public interest in the assassination of President Kennedy and its interlocking connection to the murder of his brother Robert. The impact of these two murders on history and the United States cannot be underestimated.

As for his art, George Mettler makes the following statement:

ART GALLERY: ROGUES AND HEROES

I am a writer who paints. A storyteller, I make pictures with pen and brush. My style and subject matter are as eclectic as my life experience. Much of my work depicts life as I have known it. My work is visceral. I see or hear something and experience an emotion, then I describe and explain it. When I am successful others also experience the emotion, recognize it, share it. Then I know I have done my job